T0399947

# A Practical Guide to Becoming a Community College President

This practical resource helps aspiring leaders demystify the challenges associated with becoming a community college president.

Building on existing scholarship and research related to historical origins of the community college, this book explores the role and function of the presidency, discusses existing demographics and the importance of meeting the needs of a diverse student population, and unpacks the required competencies and leadership challenges related to becoming a community college president.

Including real voices from award-winning and current presidents as well as a step-by-step approach to attaining the position, this is an important resource that speaks to the needs of today and tomorrows' community college leaders.

**Edward J. Valeau, Author**, is Superintendent President Emeritus of Hartnell Community College, California, USA.

**Rosalind Latiner Raby, Contributing Editor**, is Senior Lecturer in the Department of Educational Leadership and Policy Studies, California State University, Northridge, USA.

# A Practical Guide to Becoming a Community College President

Edward J. Valeau

Rosalind Latiner Raby,
Contributing Editor

NEW YORK AND LONDON

First published 2021
by Routledge
605 Third Avenue, New York, NY 10158

and by Routledge
2 Park Square, Milton Park, Abingdon, Oxon, OX14 4RN

*Routledge is an imprint of the Taylor & Francis Group, an informa business*



*Library of Congress Cataloging-in-Publication Data*
Names: Valeau, Edward James, author. | Latiner Raby, Rosalind, editor.
Title: A practical guide to becoming a community college president / Edward J. Valeau with Contributing Editor Rosalind Latiner Raby.
Identifiers: LCCN 2020053502 (print) | LCCN 2020053503 (ebook) | ISBN 9780367530440 (hardback) | ISBN 9780367533519 (paperback) | ISBN 9781003081555 (ebook)
Subjects: LCSH: Community college presidents. | Community colleges—Administration. | Community colleges—History. | Educational leadership.
Classification: LCC LB2341 .V28 2021 (print) | LCC LB2341 (ebook) | DDC 378.1/11—dc23
LC record available at https://lccn.loc.gov/2020053502
LC ebook record available at https://lccn.loc.gov/2020053503

ISBN: 978-0-367-53044-0 (hbk)
ISBN: 978-0-367-53351-9 (pbk)
ISBN: 978-1-003-08155-5 (ebk)

Typeset in Sabon
by codeMantra

# Dedication

This book is dedicated to my mother and father for their love, comfort, and instilling in me the value and importance of family, a strong work ethic, and a sense of self-confidence; they have guided my entire life. To my nine brothers and sisters who cared for and guided me in my formative years. I proudly stand on their shoulders and give thanks for their love. I owe Mrs. Delores Henderson, my high school English teacher, first mentor, and guardian angel who entered me into Southern University, Baton Rouge, Louisiana; she altered my life course. To all my mentors, notably Roger E. Winston, Doris M. Ward, Del M. Anderson, Linda Salter, AR DeHart, John Petersen, and my UC Berkley Professor and Dissertation Chair, Dale E. Tillery. Dale provided me with counsel, direction, and support during my studies. He significantly impacted my preparation for and ascendancy to a leadership role in the community college. To my son and most trusted friend Dwayne E. Valeau, whose loving care is my eternal blessing, pride, and joy. Finally, to my wife, friend, confidant, traveling companion, partner, and love of my life, Mrs. Vera C. Valeau. Her name is written on every line and page of my life story. She inspires me to soar.

# Contents

# Foreword

Dr. Ed Valeau is an active and important leader in American Community Colleges, having the experience and knowledge from more than 35 years of valuable service. Dr. Valeau has been central to the career development, mentoring, and placement of literally hundreds of community college presidents. I have worked with Ed as he conducted searches and facilitated presidents' selection in community college districts, where I served as Chancellor. Ed Valeau is a well-known, respected community college leader admired by his colleagues, and his many contributions represent important milestones in the evolution of many California Community Colleges.

California has changed dramatically since its first community college campus opened in Fresno in 1910. Life since 1910 has become increasingly complex, stressful, and demanding. California workers have transitioned from an agrarian and industrial state to include workers in the space age, information/knowledge state of today's global economy.

Serving as a community college president in California requires managing a wide array of issues and opportunities. California Community College presidents manage and lead in the center of the changes that are occurring in the "world of work." Community colleges provide much of the labor force in education, commerce, government, entertainment, technology, and health care. Given the sweeping social pressures and the rumbling shifts in the digitized global economy, California Community College leaders must cope with both complex challenges and extraordinary opportunities. In this book, Ed Valeau identifies and explains the pathway essential for a committed leader who has the desire and capability to work toward and succeed in becoming president of a 21st-century community college.

The past is a prologue and is a foundation for a breathtakingly different future. In technology, for example, 5G digital and neuro-technology are exploding our digital and robotic world. California will be in the center of this coming work-altering explosion. Community colleges will be central in providing the essential labor and professional service that is the essence of the California economy. Technical occupations such as agri-business, airframe, power, solar, bookkeeping, accounting, nursing, exotic animal management training, environmental science, political science, and more will be at the center of surging change. More than 50% of the members of the California legislature attended community colleges. More than 70% of returning veterans attend community colleges. Most nurses in California come from community colleges. Most of the first-generation and immigrant citizens attend community colleges. Community colleges are recognized as a big part of an answer to the rising tuition concerns yet. Moreover, the community colleges are central to each community's public needs in which they are located.

Community colleges offer quality education and are increasingly acknowledged as the best educational step forward for high school graduates and adults pursuing careers or interested in continuing their higher education. Community colleges are complex and offer diverse types of programs. Dr. Valeau emphasizes that the steps to the presidency require a commitment to fairness, integrity, service, human dignity, inner strength, and a willingness to adapt to the opportunities that change brings creatively. Applying Ed Valeau's pathways gives aspiring leaders the necessary formula for achieving career success. The choices to lead requires the strength of personality, administrative talent, and creativity.

*A Practical Guide to Becoming a Community College President* is a professionally written, clearly articulated formula necessary to achieve a presidency. This important book summarizes what has happened in the past century and offers a blueprint for leaders to "pay it forward." The case studies show the accomplishments of key leaders as examples for how their pathways influenced their leadership styles. The conclusions emphasize significantly changing practices and new career opportunities in moving forward.

The California Community Colleges provide a substantial portion of the occupational, technical, and professional labor force in California. The University of California is now giving emphasis to the Transfer Admissions Guarantee (TAG) program at the University of California and the Associate Degree Transfer (ADT) program for California State University transfers. Community college transfers are central to necessary vertical P-20 articulation that is historical in California. The phenomenally successful and effective Master Plan for Higher Education, originally launched in 1963, is now rapidly changing, adapting, and evolving. The practical guide includes examples of the competencies necessary for career advancement for those who aspire to become a community college president or chancellor.

Having taught in seven of the California doctoral programs emphasizing educational leadership and served as a mentor to successful community college leaders, I believe that this book is an important read for aspiring community college professionals enrolled in 21st-century community college leadership programs. *A Practical Guide to Becoming a Community College President* is a stargate leading to career advancement. Those who read, accept, and follow the guidelines will benefit as they thoughtfully travel a well-conceived pathway to the presidency. It is an essential read.

Bernard Luskin, Ed.D.
*Past Chair, American Association of Community Colleges*
*Director, Kellogg Community College Leadership Legacy Project*
*Community College Chancellor/President, Emeritus*
*Faculty, Community College Project, University of California, Los Angeles*

# Foreword

*A Practical Guide to Becoming a Community College President* is an excellent combination of professional development insights and leadership strategies necessary for survival. This book is not just about leadership, getting the job, or keeping it; it is also about what the journey entails in transit to the presidency. It is also an enthusiastic celebration of the unique role that community colleges play in higher education. Finally, it is a unique tribute to a select group of community college leaders who made significant contributions to the community college sector.

Another inspiring element of the book is provided by captivating historical vignettes that are interwoven in Chapter 1: Historical Footprints and Chapter 2: Ancient Roots of the College President and a Contemporary Genera. In our view, too many community college professionals are unaware of the unique history and importance of the Community College Movement. These two chapters provide valuable information that will be valuable for those in leadership roles and those aspiring for leadership roles in the community college.

We encourage readers to pay close attention to the advice provided by the author and to learn as much as possible about issues such as participatory governance, where to find help dealing with change, and team building and development. It is also essential for new presidents to negotiate a proper employment contract to work with the board to develop expectations and goals for the first year, and to know what not to do in the first year (office remodeling, expensive inaugurations, etc.), and to be mindful about picking the battles (Do not take on too much change).

Still, another element of the book is provided by richness of the case studies and the interviews with distinguished retired and sitting CEOs who represent a cross-section of racially, ethnically, and gender-based presidents. Their stories illustrated the multifaceted qualifications and competencies of community college leaders.

Although the emphasis of this book is the community college presidency, it contains much that will be of interest to those outside the CEO role in any leadership capacity. Dr. Valeau reminds the reader that individuals interested in becoming a college president should understand that the community college presidency is not for everyone. It is essential to take an assessment of the requirements for the position and the competencies that one brings to the position. Ask the question: Is this presidency a good fit? The author explains why it is essential to do homework on the job by finding out what the issues are before the final interview. We think that Valeau can be confident that readers will have gained a broader perspective of the steps to the presidency as a result of his efforts.

Most leaders understand that effective leadership in higher education is becoming increasingly dependent on leaders with varied skill sets. Team development is one of the skills that everyone knows successful leaders should possess, but most are not aware of the finer details that go into everyday practical leadership and building strong teams. Our books, *Practical Leadership in Community Colleges: Navigating Today's Challenges* (2016) and *Team Leadership in Community Colleges* (2019), address the topics of strengthening everyday leadership skills and how to collaborate with teams to manage and transform community Colleges. In this book, Valeau continues the conversation about collaborating with teams by stating:

> New presidents must have the ability to build a diverse team of people with different skills, knowledge, and abilities. Also, they must be diverse in age, race, ethnicity, and gender. Finally, the CEO must be skilled in molding the team into a functional team that complements and supports each other. (p. 52)

This book provides a valuable window to insights on the pursuit of the presidency and the competencies needed to get and sustain the position. The challenges in community college leadership are both problematic and fascinating. Community college leaders, associations, and leadership preparation programs are working with enthusiasm and dedication to prepare the next generation of community college leaders. In this new age of leading community colleges, it is necessary to provide community college practitioners, both current leaders and emerging leaders, with state-of-the-art knowledge on the past and frontiers in leadership strategies. *This book* is a good step in that direction.

George R. Boggs and Christine Johnson McPhail

# Preface

During my tenure as a Community College CEO and as cofounder of a successful national CEO executive search firm, I have received many questions from aspiring leaders. Four of these questions help to guide this book:

- How do I become a community college president?
- Are there special avenues and keys that open the door?
- Do I have the right stuff?
- Am I the fit they are looking for?

The number of materials surrounding the above questions is voluminous. It spreads across books, dissertations, articles, and chapters covering the span of community college history. This makes it virtually impossible for aspiring leaders to assimilate all the information and factor it into their journey as many are full-time employees. Future leaders are bombarded with the job's everyday work and need a resource that is based in fact, easily digestible, and applicable in real-time. The purpose of this book is to help demystify the process, offer concrete steps to alleviate misconceptions and frustrations prompted by the questions above, and provide the reader with guideposts on their journey to the position.

This book is not intended to be exhaustive. It does not suggest one size fits all. The job is far too complicated; the environments are too varied. The personality and preparation of each aspirant are as unique as are the colleges they hope to lead. Such factors contribute heavily to why there is no cookie-cutter recipe for securing the presidency. Instead, this book is designed to help aspiring leaders unpack the role and delve deep into what is required. It is intended to reveal the challenges and opportunities presented by the role, what leaders are likely to face in carrying out their roles, and strategies for managing their journey up to and out of the job. I hope to identify pathways that will enlighten aspirants and policymakers inside and outside of the colleges that while the road to the presidency is strenuous and challenging, it is possible for those committed to and willing to work hard to have a rewarding and fulfilling career. It is particularly essential as colleges continue to experience high turnover rates. Equally important is a need for a diverse body of leaders who can best serve the needs of a student body that is mostly people of color and women.

In particular, the book builds on existing scholarship related to historical origins of the community college; the title, role, and function of the presidency; existing demographics; challenges related to diversifying the ranks to meet the needs of a diverse student population; and required competencies and leadership challenges related to being a community college president, the position, and its effectiveness. The book also uses case studies and interviews with prominent retired CEOs and a cross-section of racially, ethnically, and gender-based sitting presidents to demonstrate the requirements needed to serve in the role and steps to get there and issues and concerns. The interviewees share their stories through the case studies and interviews and offer wise counsel and advice to aspiring leaders interested in serving as presidents. While the book presents concrete steps to the presidency, leaders interested in becoming a college president should understand, one size does not fit all. The journey is arduous, time-consuming, nerve-wracking, lengthy, and filled with many winding roads and stops that only the aspirant can walk.

Written by a former community college president with more than 35 years of experience in college administration, author, and CEO Executive Search Consultant, the book provides readers with a close and personal view of the presidency, aspects of performing with distinction while understanding and mastering the rules of the road, elements of a job description and how to read it, role and work of the screening committee, important information for constructing a successful cover letter and resume, and suggestions on how to manage the interview process skillfully. Combined, it offers some convincing evidence for what can be viewed as guided pathways based on an inside view of the steps an individual may pursue and achieve the community college presidency.

Higher education presidents are pivotal to the success of colleges and universities. It is particularly true for community colleges that have long been championed as the people's college. These colleges are generally located in the community where taxpayers have expressed a specific interest in having a source for higher education that addresses community needs, business interests, and the need for an educated and trained citizenry.

Presidents leading community colleges are linked to traditionally disenfranchised aspirants and have responsibility for assuring that all students who can profit from higher education have every opportunity to do so. They guide the "the people's colleges" that turn people's dreams to reality on every level imaginable.

Through their effort, community college presidents ensure that their campuses are a laboratory for teaching and learning. They engage the faculty with the idea of supporting them for innovating teaching and learning practices. They work with politicians and local leaders to secure funding for innovative programming and practices to ensure relevance; they are sensitive to and in tune with their student body's diversity. They are aware that they are the first generation of enrollees looking for an opportunity to become the best they can be. These presidents have generally chosen the community college as their leadership pathway to make a difference in the students' lives and the communities they serve. Unlike University presidents, community college presidents are likely to have traditionally worked their way up through student services or instruction. Many have attended a community college as their first institution of higher education, putting them closer to the students and communities they serve.

Becoming a community college president is an arduous task. It requires years of consistent preparation that involves studying the role of the community college, understanding its long and storied history, learning about the social and political trends and circumstances that dictate the ability of the college to serve its students, and having a passion for working with the student bodies that are likely enrolled. Evidence exists to show that most students enrolled in community colleges are people of color and women. Their participation demands attention related to creative, innovative, and relevant training, appropriate counseling, mentoring, and support that results in access and success. Community college presidents are not shielded from the community they serve but rather an integral part, thus the current use "community college." They could be called the peoples' president.

Embarking on a career as a community college president demands that aspirants be committed to bold and courageous leadership. It demands that aspirants have the competencies to lead an institution through its ups and downs while striving for greatness. Community college presidents are expected to be visionaries, innovators, and builders of people, programs, services, and students. They are required to manage the college or district affairs and work cooperatively and communicate effectively with all constituents. Issues of the day related to budgeting and financing, curricular and student services planning, fundraising, student life, community needs, and business and industry needs all fall with the role's scope. At any time, the president can be an enemy or friend depending on what she did not or did grant. It is likely the complexity of the job will increase, and thus there is a need for aspirants to know the pathways to the presidency and to have the mysteries of how to become one uncovered in a plain and simple manner.

This book is intended for aspiring leaders interested in the role of CEO and the identification of competencies needed to perform successfully. It is also for those working in community colleges who find themselves on the leadership pathway even if that was not their intent. The book is also for graduate students and universities engaged in preparing future leaders for the presidency. It is a resource for schools growing their own leaders, mentors assisting aspiring leaders, and Boards of Trustees with responsibility for hiring CEOs. Finally, it is targeted to associations working to prepare leaders for a role as president.

In sum, this book looks back at the past and learns from the present in preparation for the future. Written by a former community college president with more than 35 years of experience in college administration, author, and CEO Executive Search Consultant, this book provides readers with a close and personal view of the presidency, aspects of performing with distinction while understanding and mastering the rules of the road, elements of a job description and how to read it, role and work of the screening committee, important information for constructing a successful cover letter and resume, and suggestions on how to manage the interview process skillfully.

## ORGANIZATIONAL STRUCTURE

This book is organized into five parts and contains chapters that help expand each part. Part I introduces the reader to the community College movement concept. *Chapter 1* identifies historical community college footprints to show its early development, growth, and expansion through legislation, policy development, and innovative programming. It reinvented itself to meet the needs of the day. *Chapter 2* points out that the higher education presidency owes its existence to the church with roots in the chancellery. It demonstrates that the presidency arose from secondary school as it mirrored the university's patterns and evolved to serve the community's needs. *Chapter 3* examines the origins of the titles Chancellor and President and looks at the first change of the role from student care to institutional issues related to budgets, finance, and curricula. *Chapter 4* highlights the characteristics of multiple generations of community college presidents, starting from around 1940 and ending in 2020. It reveals the profiles of presidents who were mostly white males and how they ascended to the role. It helps shed some light on the often-asked question: What do I need to do to get the role? *Chapter 5* introduces the readers to the community colleges' student and faculty profiles, noting a disconnect between a student body populated by people of color and women and the teaching faculty and administrators recruited to serve them. It reveals that the gains in diversity have been minimal and continue to move very slowly.

In Part II, building leverages to get the job, the reader is introduced briefly to elements associated with climbing the ladder to the top. *Chapter 6* briefly explains the historical pathways to the presidency, including leadership pathways, the importance of terminal degrees, relevant experience, training, and mentoring. *Chapter 7* provides elements essential to understanding the job. It reveals the presidents' demands, including the board of trustees' faculty, faculty staff, students, and the community. *Chapter 8* identifies the value of networking, the importance of developing a network, and how difficult it is to cultivate one. *Chapter 9* discusses how institutions conduct the interview process from beginning to end. *Chapter 10* outlines the elements of a typical job announcement explaining a district's position, characteristics, and description of the college within a district. The chapter also provides insight into how a job description is formed and the planning and time that goes into the process.

Part III outlines lived stories from the field to delve deeper into aspirants' feelings and former and sitting Community College presidents' attitudes and behavior. *Chapter 11* is based on interviews with distinguished leaders referred to as Buttimer Award recipients of the Association of California Community College Administrators. They are former CEOs and recognized as outstanding leaders in California Community colleges, the nation's most extensive system of Community colleges. The award is quite prestigious and offered once a year to a recognized recipient. The chapter explains this cohort's journey, including their preparation, motivation, and recommendations for success in the president's role. *Chapter 12* presents a profile of selected community college presidents that are racially, ethnically, and gendered diverse. The reader is guided through their journey to witness the execution of the role through enduring challenges in preparation, role function, leadership styles, and the management of expectations; and how important it is to maintain your personal compass as a guide. *Chapter 13* presents a comparative analysis of the similarities and differences between Buttimer award recipients and Sitting presidents. It demonstrates how time and situation dictate leadership, how styles vary, and the meaning of different leaders' jobs. *Chapter 14* presents a case study to show the evolution of a CEO and how unforeseen activities can contribute to securing a role as president. It is a personal reflection that can resonate with the readers' own experiences.

Part IV discusses aspirants' competencies in the future and what they must do to keep their jobs. *Chapter 15* presents the readers with some guided pathways for building 21st-Century Competencies that include understanding the context of the job, having a desire for the job and what it entails, acquiring the needed experience and skills to do the job, obtaining the terminal degree, securing a mentor, cultivating a network, and acquiring advanced training. It also points out that this does not guarantee you a role but positions you to be competitive in an increasingly complex field. *Chapter 16* discusses how important it is to have a philosophy and the strength and courage to embrace the role and all that goes with it wholeheartedly. The chapter encourages leaders to find their voice and manage the stress associated with being in the leadership role.

Part V provides the readers with a futuristic view of the presidency. *Chapter 17* explains that colleges of the future will be dominated by people of color and the need for changing the profile of community college presidents now, and that the needle showing change is too slow or stuck. It emphasizes that leaders require, among other things, increased sensitivity to the social ills governing the communities they serve and focused involvement in creating sustainable vision and activities that address student learning, technology, training, and equity. Finally, *Chapter 18* discusses why there is no mystery to ascending to the presidency and outlines what readers should take away from this book.

# Acknowledgments

I much appreciate and thank those colleagues who served as peer readers and gave their time and critical assessments of the strengths and weaknesses of the manuscript. Their effort helped to bring this book to fruition. Thanks to those sitting and retired presidents who participated in the interviews and took the surveys to provide deep insight into the views and concerns of a college president's role and function and the challenges they face as they strive to lead their organization's needs to achieve success. Thanks to Bernie Luskin, who was the first to encourage my effort, including support to get it published. He reminded me that I had something good, but it would take time to complete. Special thanks to Sherry Culver and Cynthia Clower, my friends and administrative assistants who typed the first thoughts, Cicely McCreight's initial edits, and Mary Grace (MJ), who got the document ready for Headley Office Services who prepared the manuscript for submission to the editors. I especially want to thank the first peer readers, Stu Sutin, Craig Follins, Daniel Derrico, Augie Gallegos, Belle Wheelan, Kathleen Rose, Marjorie Lewis, Barbara Wright-Sanders, Fran White, Tom Van Gronigen, Judy Walters, and Charles Ratliff who paved the way for further expansion and development of the manuscript. Special thanks to George Boggs and Christine McPhail, who are not only friends but longtime collaborators and whose influence has been impactful on me.

Moreover, I owe thanks to Uttam Gaulle and Krishna Bista for opening doors to this book's publication and believing in my efforts. Finally, I want to acknowledge Rosalind Latiner Raby, my friend and co-author on several books, for her standards of excellence, encouragement, and a keen eye for details. Her outstanding editing and sense of organization greatly influenced the book's completion, which could not have been done without her. Her support was the glue needed to complete this book. She has my love and enduring appreciation and admiration. Moreover, I extend thanks to my colleagues and friends who took the time to comment on the book's value.

# Illustrations

## FIGURES



## TABLES

Part I

# Introduction to the Community College: Historical Footprints

Chapter One

# Historical Footprints

The community college, thought to be an American invention, actually had its roots in selected institutions worldwide (Raby & Valeau, 2007). The United States version of the community college has a rich and colorful history that is poorly understood generally by politicians, educators, and the public. Some stalwarts (Brubacher & Rudy, 1976; Cohen & Brawer, 2008; Rudolph, 1962) have provided a historical and comprehensive context for the field. It is important to chronicle the community college movement's historical evolution because the past informs the present's actions, thus shaping the future. Essential for this book is that through understanding the past, future leaders can cultivate an understanding and appreciation for the community college movement's complexity and the need for leaders who can effectively and successfully lead the community colleges of today and tomorrow. Understanding the community college movement is useful to future leaders, as it can help them avoid old mistakes when working with the college community to create new opportunities and visions. The community college's ever-changing nature forces leaders to develop a critical understanding of where the community college has been, where it is now, and where it needs to serve all its constituents effectively.

While many authors help inform the outline below, I was informed most by George Vaughn (1995), a pioneer in the field who helped define and chronicle the movement in the last half century. However, history is told differently in different time periods, and as such, I also used multiple sources to add updates and commentary.

## 1850–1900

1862 – *Passage of the Morrill Act*, often referred to as the Land Grant Act, expanded access to public higher education, teaching both courses and students previously excluded from higher education. The Morrill Act is vital for community colleges because it influenced the founding in 1901 of the first junior college in Joliet, Illinois. This two-year program is often considered a prototype for today's community colleges.

1890 – *Passage of the Second Morrill Act* withheld funds from any state that refused admission to the land-grant colleges based on race, unless the states provided separate institutions for minorities. As a result, public higher education opportunities began to be open to all students. It is essential for community colleges because it offered options for all students of all social classes to take vocational training, workforce training, and adult education as we know it today.

## 1900–1950

1901 – The founding of the oldest public junior college, Joliet Junior College in Illinois, was greatly influenced by the educational vision of William Rainey Harper, President of the University of Chicago.

1904 – The "*Wisconsin Idea*," created by the University of Wisconsin, used the university to assist the public through extension services and assistance to the state government. The university declared the boundaries of the state to be its campus. It also created an opportunity for staff and students to work, discover, and discuss ideas together in a shared community. It was vital for community colleges, as it made it possible for every citizen of Wisconsin to benefit from knowledge and discoveries created at the university and, by extension, others in the nation and the world.

1907–1917 – California Legislation authorized high schools to offer postgraduate courses and then provided state and county support for students who attended junior college branches. Finally, the state provided independent junior college districts with their boards, budgets, and procedures. The Community College Department in Fresno Unified School District was established in 1907.

1920–1921 – Founding of the *American Association of Junior Colleges* (AAJC). Three inaugural meetings were held in St. Louis (June 30–July 1, 1920), St. Louis (June 30–July 1, 1921), and Chicago (February 1921). The AAJC mission was to provide a national focus and national leadership for the nation's Community, Junior, and Technical colleges. George Zook was the first elected Executive Director.

1928 – The *Junior College Movement* (1928) by Leonard Koos described the development of the public junior college, emphasizing geographic distribution, enrollments, and study programs. He was editor of University of Chicago's *School Review*, and was considered the farthest authority on junior college development.

**1931** – *The Junior College* (1931) by Walter Crosby Eells documented the public junior college's growth and curriculum and underscored its role in increasing access to higher education. He served as the Executive Secretary of the AAJC and then became the Secretary of the American Association of Research Colleges, where he served until 1946.

**1944** – *The Servicemen's Readjustment Act*, known as *the GI Bill*, was passed, which provided financial assistance for veterans who wished to pursue higher education. The GI Bill gave veterans access to a variety of institutions from community colleges to Ivy League universities. It created a particular area for veterans and created a new population of students and learning and service challenges.

**1946** – Jesse Bogue became the executive secretary of the AAJC, a position he held until 1958. Bogue popularized the term "community college" in his book *The Community College* (1950). In the years following, most existing junior colleges and new public two-year colleges began to use the term "community" in their names.

**1946** – *President Truman's Commission on Higher Education* published *Higher Education for American Democracy* (Zook, 1947), which established a network of public community colleges that would charge little or no tuition, serve as cultural centers, be comprehensive in their program offerings with an emphasis on civic responsibilities, and would serve the area in which they were located. Included in this document was the validation of international education's importance to community colleges, including their mission, academic and technical programs, and community outreach.

## 1950–2000

**1958** – Edmund J. Gleazer, Jr. became the AAJC's Executive Director, the title that replaced "Executive Secretary." In 1972, the title was once again changed to President. Gleazer remained in his position until 1981.

**1960** – *The Junior College Leadership Program* (JCLP) was established at 12 universities funded by the W.K. Kellogg Foundation. The Kellogg Fellowships were prestigious appointments and recognized as central to the development of community college leadership. They provided a significant career trajectory for the more than 500 recipients, and as such, the JCLP ended up educating the next generation of deans and presidents. Through the JCLP, junior colleges become core community assets through programs designed to broaden these institutions academically while encouraging them to become more responsive to their communities' needs. In turn, the comprehensive community college model was reinforced and revised for this new generation.

**1960** – *The Junior College: Progress and Prospect* (1960) by Leland Medsker outlined the strengths and weaknesses of the public community college, including data on students' academic performance and transfer success in selected states. The study outlined the junior college's strengths as expanding access for a diverse student population, providing preparatory curricula to advance undergraduate education in the four-year university, and offering a wide range of general and specialized courses for adult learners. The book also detailed the weaknesses, including underfunding, delegation as a low-status institution, and focus on being a holding place for those students unable or unwilling to enter a four-year college.

**1963** – The first computer was installed at Orange Coast College, CA, which built the foundation for future information systems adopted nationwide. The *Education Professions Development Act* offered teacher education workshops to train the early computer technology faculty cohort.

**1964** – President Lyndon Johnson signed the *Civil Rights Act of 1964*, which supported increased diversity in public education by linking federal funding for student aid based on diversity numbers. The Civil Rights Act directly impacted community colleges' enrollment of underrepresented students.

**1967** – Dr. Joseph Cosand, Superintendent/President of the St. Louis Community College District, adopted the title Chancellor to make the statement that community colleges are part of higher education. It started the wave in use of the title Chancellor and Vice-Chancellor.

**1968** – The first community college Education Abroad courses were offered at Cabrillo Community College (CA), Glendale Community College (CA), and Rockland Community college (NY). These courses showed that while the community college serves the students who reside in a local region, the curriculum and the instruction mode's location are not limited.

**1970** – Orange Coast Jr. College District (CA) launched KOCE-TV, a Public Television Station owned by the district that produced telecourses. Together with Miami-Dade (FL) and Dallas (TX), these courses helped trigger the telecourse movement, a precursor of today's online courses. Like the education abroad courses, these courses helped to blur the geographic boundaries of the community college.

**1972** – *The California Commission on Higher Education Project Outreach* (1972) led to legislation allowing public funds to be used for instruction outside the classroom. It expanded opportunities for adults and continuing higher education, lifelong learning, and coordinated extended degree programs between higher education segments. The California Commission also enacted State legislation (Section 23754) that authorized waivers for specified percentages of international students to attend California State University and California Community Colleges.

**1976** – Coastline Community College (CA) launched the first community college without walls, using telecourses and community colleges, leading the way to substantially increase diversity in offerings and attract a new cohort of students.

**1965/1972/1992** – *The Higher Education Act of 1965, the 1972 amendment, and the 1992 higher education amendment and federal Pell Grant* made it possible for almost all Americans to attend college. It is important, since it widened the doors for community colleges to serve poor and minoritized students by institutionalizing support through financial aid, scholarships, and work-study.

**1972** – The education amendments of the Higher Education Act of 1965 were amended to include Title IX. Title IX provided a procedural basis for handling sexual harassment incidents and prohibited discrimination based on sex that significantly affected athletic programs and team sports in community colleges and higher education in general.

**1981** – Dale Parnell became President of AACJC and served until 1991. Parnell was the first AACJC President to have been a president of a public community college. During his tenure, the association established a press and issued a newspaper, the *Community College Times*.

**1988** – *Report of the Commission on the Future of Community Colleges, Building Communities: A Vision for a New Century* (AACC, 1988), commissioned by the American Association of Community Colleges (AACC), defined *community* not only as a region to be served but as a climate to be created. It supported noninstructional ways of *building community* on-campus, including orientation programs, student support services, and programs aimed to break down barriers based on age, race, or ethnicity, development of global/international awareness programs, and service-learning programs. The Commission also identified four academic goals to be pursued within the community college curriculum: (1) literacy for all students, (2) a core of common learning, (3) preparation for work, and (4) education for lifelong learning.

**1991** – David Pierce became President of AACJC and was the first president to have graduated from a public community college. In his tenure, he emphasized working with the federal government, especially the education and labor departments, and interpreting the community college's mission to both national and international audiences.

**1995** – *American Association of Community Colleges* (AACC) changed its name. The AACJC dropped the Junior because it was a name of lesser quality and changed its name to the AACC.

## 2000–2020

2001 – Community colleges celebrated 100 years of service.

2001 – Nationwide, community colleges began to offer the practical baccalaureate degree to meet the local workforce's changing needs and support more diverse students in their efforts to gain a BA degree. The first applied baccalaureate program was offered in 1992.

2004 – Launch of the national *Achieving the Dream: Community Colleges Count Initiative*. This initiative was an effort to improve student completion rates supported by the Lumina Foundation. The initiative's goal is to help more community college students succeed, especially students of color, working adults, and students from low-income families.

2004 – The League for Innovation in the Community College published a White Paper called *An Assessment Framework for the Community College*. The focus of this paper was on building common assessment techniques that were aimed at improving student success.

2006 – Salmon Khan created the *Khan Academy*, a nonprofit Open Educational Resource organization that offered free online tutorials via videos to practice exercises and a personalized learning dashboard that empowers learners to study at their own pace in and out of the classroom. The Khan Academy partners with the community college to help students prepare for placement exams and remedial development.

2007 – Forty-seven states adopted a system for reporting performance data to improve accountability and to support short- and long-range planning to serve students. It was greatly influenced by accrediting agencies across the country who sought to streamline community colleges' institution quality.

2009 – *American Graduation Initiative program*, launched by the President Obama administration, aimed to have the highest proportion of college graduates in the world by 2020. Financial support to institutions based on accountability and financial support to students were provided.

2010 – The Obama Administration held the first summit on the community college to recognize its achievement and announce support programs.

2010 – The Aspen Institute began to offer a *College Excellent Program Award* to community colleges based on their achievements in fostering student success. The monetary awards have since become the nation's signature recognition of high achievement and performance.

2012 – Udacity began offering 11 free online courses, following the MOOC (Massive Open Online Class) model. It worked in cooperation with community colleges to provide another tool for online learning.

2012 – Almost 50% of the first-time undergraduates began their post-secondary career at a community college.

2012 – Harvard, MIT, and UC Berkeley partnered to offer free online classes that validated the value of online education and allowed students to take online courses at prestigious institutions. It also allowed the community colleges to expand their relationship and online program with such prestigious institutions that opened new transfer possibilities.

2015 – President Obama unveiled the *American College Promise* program, a plan to make two years of a community college education available free of charge to "everyone willing to work for it."

2017 – Tennessee became the first state to offer free community college to nearly every adult. It has since been joined in some form by other states, including Arkansas, California, Delaware, Georgia, Indiana, Kentucky, Maryland, Nevada, New Jersey, New York, Oregon, Rhode Island, and Tennessee.

2020 – Community colleges dealt with COVID-19 and the aftermath of the economic recession. #BlackLivesMatter renews and accelerates conversations for equity and social justice.

2020 – The California Community College Equity Leadership Alliance was created with over 50 California community college presidents. They pledged to provide resources, training, and annual assessments to its members, all aimed at improving equity by working against racism in all its forms, including implicit bias and prominent racist practices. The focus is to stand together to be anti-racist (St. Amour, 2020).

2020 – The effects of the COVID-19 pandemic were intense and unforgiving. The human toll has been staggering, and the long-term economic effects will be felt for years to come. Higher educational changes were made in terms of altered teaching modalities, refocused curriculum, on-line learning and interrupted services.

2020 – Disruptions to International Student programs. On May 29, President Trump suspended entry of specific students and researchers from selected countries, which resulted in thousands of students not returning to the United States to complete their studies. In July, the Trump administration forbade online instruction for international students and threatened deportation for those living in the United States. Although that policy was rescinded, the stability of international student programs is uncertain. It will result in a significant financial loss for community colleges that would be in the hundreds of millions.

## REFERENCES

American Association of Community Colleges (AACC). (1988) *Commission on the future of community colleges. Building communities: A vision for a new century*. AACC.

Bogue, J. (1950). *The community college*. McGraw Hill.

Brubacher, J. S., & Rudy W. (1976). *Higher education in transition: A history of American Colleges and Universities, 1963–1976* (3rd ed.). Routledge.

Cohen, A. M., & Brawer, F. B. (2008). *The American community college.* Jossey-Bass.

Eells, W. C. (1931). *The junior college.* Houghton Mifflin.

Koos, L. (1928). *Junior college movement.* Gin and Company.

League for Innovation in the Community College. (2004). White paper: An assessment framework for the community college. https://www.league.org/sites/default/files/An%20Assessment%20Framework%20for%20the%20Community%20College_Occasional%20Paper.pdf.

Lumina Foundation. (2004). Achieving the dream: Community colleges count initiative. http://luminafundaition.org/achievingthedream/.

Medsker, L. L. (1960). *The junior college: Progress and prospect.* https://www.ucop.edu/acadinit/astplan/MPSelectCmte1172. pdf.

Raby, R. L., & Valeau, E. J. (2007). Community college international education: Looking back to forecast the future. In *International reform efforts and challenges in community colleges. New directions for community colleges.* Edited by E. J. Valeau, & R. L. Raby (138, Summer) (pp. 5–14). Jossey-Bass.

Rudolph, F. (1962). *The American college and university: A history.* Knopf.

St. Amour, M. (2020). California''s community colleges unite on racial equity. June 12, 2020. *Inside Higher Education.* https://www.insidehighered.com/news/2020/06/12/california-community-college-alliance-aims-improve-racial-equity-higher-education?XuU8jX7Mf8V.

Vaughn, G. (1995). *The community college story: A tale of American innovation.* American Association of Community Colleges, National Center for Higher Education.

Zook, G. (1947). *The president's commission on higher education: Higher education for American democracy.* U.S. Government Printing Office.

Chapter Two

# Ancient Roots of the College President and a Contemporary Genera

To appreciate and understand the community college presidency's present concept, I first refer to its ancient roots. Charles Thwing (1926) was an early observer of the College Presidency. He opined that the President's office and title are part of a long and historical tradition characterizing the role. He also wrote about the inheritance and survival of the position that denotes the head of a community college, college, or university in the United States. This section is included to provide a brief context for aspirants to appreciate where the title Presidency originated and how it relates to their aspirations.

## HISTORIC ROOTS

Early writers (Prator, 1963; Rashdall, 1936; Schmidt, 1930; Thwing, 1926) provide a framework for the evolution of the president title with roots in the Chancellery. In medieval times, the title Chancellor was entrenched in empirical and ecclesiastical relationships and took root in educational underpinnings. The title was brought to England by Edward the Confessor (Thwing, 1926) and was given to a person responsible for charters, letters, and the sovereign's official writings. Concurrently, in the church, the Orders of the Knighthood, a powerful organization, redefined the Chancellor's role to be a broker with Episcopal responsibilities serving as the connecting link between the Pope and the University. In England, the title was also applied to the leader of four of the colleges at Oxford: Magdalene, Corpus Christi, St. John's and Trinity, and Queens College of Cambridge. In Oxford and Cambridge, the Chancellor had full authority and, over time, emerged to become a chief executive officer (CEO) and became what is commonly used in colleges today, a role as head of a college or university system. Likewise, today, the Chancellor of a community college reports to a Board of Trustees responsible for an entire district's overall leadership, suggesting a larger span of control, power, and influence.

The Rector title had its roots in Italy in the 12th century. It was applied to civil officers and officers of the guild. Universities adopted the term, first as an honorary term and later to represent the head of faculties and took precedence over Deans and proctors. Eventually, the term emerged to become the formal president or head of the university. It is not a term currently used at community colleges.

The term Principal was first used in 1509 at Brasenose Oxford and was particularly common to denote senior leadership in women's colleges. Initially, in British higher education, principals were appointed by the crown, and some were appointed for life. In the absence of a Chancellor and Rector, the Principal served as Chairman of the University and general counsel. The Principal could be appointed by the Chancellor to serve as Vice-Chancellor in the Chancellor's absence. Last century, in the United States, the term Principal was mostly given to the head of a high school or secondary-level academy. However, it was also given to the first generation of community college leadership.

The Provost title grew out of the church and was initially given to a chief officer in a cathedral church. The Provost was second to the abbot in the school rankings. The Provost has become a secondary position in colleges and universities in the United States, with varying responsibilities and duties that may or not be related to staff in nature. In the community college, and in some cases, it has become akin to a vice presidency and is often a stepping-stone to higher community college leadership positions, including the presidency.

The terms Chancellor, Rector, Provost, and Principal show a universal acceptance to designate higher education institutions' chief head. These various terms also indicate inconsistencies in defining leadership roles in higher education.

## US COMMUNITY COLLEGE PRESIDENCY

The US community college President generally arose from the secondary school sector. The first generation of community college presidents came from school principals and school superintendents. These individuals migrated to the community college because of their experiences as leaders in the secondary school system (Piland & Wolf 2003). As noted previously, the community college has its roots in the K-12 system. As such, the adoption of school leadership constructs was in continuity with the community college's development. Within the first generation of Junior Colleges, the secondary leadership role was merged with that of the university leadership role. In this Generation, the junior college presidents created the tenets of what is expected of a president. Like today, this included forming a vision, articulating the college's needs, serving the constituencies' needs, and leading the college to effectively achieve its mission.

As the junior college morphed into the current community college, the President's role changed from having significant responsibility for developing student character in overseeing student services and later for student success in broader contexts. Senior administrative offices changed from instruction to offices of instruction, from finance to chief business officer, and from personnel to the office of human relations. Over time, other organizational units appeared within the institution for distinct purposes and adopted to help relieve the President's burden. New offices were created that included such titles as the Office of Student Services, Administrative Services, Office of Diversity, and International Education. This adaptation highlighted a response to changing social, economic, political, and cultural conditions that forced the community college to change by continually addressing its entire citizenry.

In 2020, the community college's top executive positions are President, Superintendent/President, and Chancellor. The Superintendent/President position is a holdover from the secondary school system, but continues as a title in some community colleges, particularly in California. The leadership task is to maintain the standards by which institutions support learning, opportunity, equity, access, and success. As leaders, they champion their institution for educational change. The President has responsibility for the institution's leadership and organization and, perchance as Chancellor, a responsibility to the Board of Trustees for its overall management and direction.

The community college presidency has been successfully adopted and specifically revised to support its mission. It is to make higher education accessible to all those who are interested and capable of profiting from or preparing to engage in a career. It aims to help people participate in the workforce and attain a higher degree or a certificate in a vocational training program of his or her choosing.

## CHANGING US COMMUNITY COLLEGE PRESIDENTIAL ROLES

The early version of the community college presidency's roles was heavily influenced by standards and conditions designed by US university presidents. Traditionally, their duties included, among other things, conducting faculty meetings, visiting classes, and promoting the interests of the college and later evolved to clarify or discover the mission of the college (Hutchinson, 1964). Cowley (1956) detailed four categories of community college presidential duties: superintending, facilitating, developing, and leading. In this context, leading was designated as different from managing and is more than administration. Included in these categories was articulating the college aims, securing others' buy-in to get them done, setting the institution's tone, providing the means to enable the staff to achieve stated goals and objectives, and supporting academic freedom. Today, the president's authority includes the ability to exercise leadership over the institution. Many variations of the role have emerged. Nevertheless, it is significantly impacted by the times, kind, needs, and structure of the organization and its geographical location.

In the current century, the president is known as the CEO, who leads a college or district serving faculty, staff, and students. The President is usually an ex-officio member of the Board of Trustees, attends all board meetings and has duties from time to time conferred upon the President by the Board of Trustees. The CEO reports to the Board on the institution's status, orally and in writing, outlining its conditions, prospects, and needs and is the instrument of contact using a participatory governance model. Equally important, the CEO represents the organization's needs and interests to the community and works with the Board as a team to support the community, students, faculty and staff, business, and industry needs. Last, the CEO signs all contracts, legal documents, obligations, and diplomas as authorized by the Board of Trustees.

The community college presidency is growing and evolving, along with institutions shifting and changing to meet the times (Beach & Grubb, 2011). Even in doing so, its tenets remain firmly in the idea and expectations of its role and function. The weight is constant. It is due in part to the demands for accountability from many constituents' groups. The Boards' expectations are consistent with yesteryears and, to some degree, higher. The presidency is an institution shrouded in history that is long, consistent, and honored. The President is the principal administrative officer responsible for a higher education institution's affairs and operations. Finally, the president is the leader and thereby is expected to lead.

## REFERENCES

Beach, J. M., & Grubb, W. N. (2011). *Gateway to opportunity: A history of the community college in the United States*. Stylus.

Cowley, W. H. (1956). What does a college president do? Presentation: Inauguration of Roy E. Lewallen as President of Oregon College of Education, Feb. 8, 18–21. ERIC.

Hutchinson, R. M. (1964). The administrator: Leader or the office holder. *Journal of Higher Education*, 16(8), 395–396.

Piland, W. E., & Wolf, D. B. (2003). *Help wanted: Preparing community college leaders in a new century*. Jossey-Bass.

Prator, R. (1963). *The college president*. Center for Applied Research in Education, Inc.

Rashdall, H. (1936). *Universities of Europe in the Middle Ages*. Oxford University Press.

Schmidt, G. P. (1930). *The old-time college president*. Columbia University Press.

Thwing, C. F. (1926). *The college president*. MacMillan.

Chapter Three

# Contemporary President Profiles

This chapter reviews the profiles of community college presidents. In this century, many presidents who have or plan to retire are demanding a refocus on training new leadership. However, the worry is that fewer leaders are interested in the job, and potential leaders are emerging from a weakened pipeline (Weltsch, 2009). It was foretold in 2001 that 86% of community college presidents were expected to retire within a decade (AACC, 2001; Shults, 2001). In 2012, 42% of a new generation of community college presidents were planning to retire in five years, and in 2017, 50% of presidents were planning to retire (Ellis & Garcia, 2017; Stripling, 2017). The aging of the presidency continues to create a context in which the percentage of those wanting to retire remains consistent (ACE, 2019; Tekle, 2012). Equally important is the increasingly short tenures of sitting Presidents. Nationally, community college presidents serve an average of six years in their position, but 38% of all presidents serve less than five years (Gagliardi et al., 2017). In some states, an average president's tenure is 3.5 years (Wheelhouse, 2016).

For over a century, community college presidents have been primarily White males (McFarlin et al., 1999; Piland & Wolf, 2003; Prator, 1963; Thwing, 1926; Wiseman & Vaughan, 1998). The *Good Old White Boy Network* concept governed the way business was conducted, the mentored, and the ultimate selection of new presidents. Three messaging activities exist that help to perpetuate this network. First, university and association leadership programs reinforce hidden messages as future leaders are taught by former presidents who taught their values and norms. In turn, a commonality of presidential traits and expectations of who can be a leader is reinforced from one generation of presidents to the next.

A second hidden message is in the portrayal of the community college president itself, which in many cases is male and White focused. McFarlin et al. (1999) described the president as:

> He is about 55 years old, has served as a community college president for 14 years. He has been at his current institution for slightly more than ten years and achieved his first community college presidency at 41 years of age. (p. 28)

Eddy and Khwaja (2019) suggest that this portrait does not acknowledge women and minorities or those with nontraditional pathways. The final example is an undercurrent of accepted male competencies and leadership norms that have long been embedded in organizational structures and leadership images that favor White Male leaders. Interestingly, some literature suggests that women and presidents of color should emulate White Male leaders (McFarlin et al., 1999). Today, the White masculine norms of leadership remain dominant in defining who leads and knows how best to lead (Eddy & Khwaja, 2019). In many contexts, women and people of color are judged against these norms (Eddy, 2009).

Consistency in demographics was captured by the Vaughan survey series administered to all US community college presidents from 1996 to 2007 (Wiseman & Vaughan, 2007). These surveys showed that presidents were getting older and not meaningfully changing in terms of their diversity. Regarding age, presidents are getting older. In 1996, most community college presidents were 54 years old, which grew to 56 in 2001, 58 in 2007, and 60 in 2012 (Eckel et al., 2009; Tekle, 2012; Wiseman & Vaughan, 2007). In 2012, Tekle found that about half of the presidents were between the ages of 55 and 64. A quarter was between the ages of 65 and 75. In 2017, community college presidents' average age grew to 67, with 20% approaching 71 years of age (Jaschik & Lederman, 2018). Another president characteristic that has mainly remained the same is that most presidents are married or have a domestic partner (ACE, 2017; Jaschik & Lederman, 2018; Wiseman & Vaughan, 2007). Newer studies are beginning to document emerging profiles, such as sexual orientation and gender preference (McNair, 2016).

In terms of race and ethnicity, only low-to-moderate gains have been achieved in the diversification of community college presidencies over the past 50 years (Stripling, 2019). It is likely due to Affirmative Action that outreach to potential leaders of color had noted payoffs (Vaughan, 1989). In 1986, 91.9% of community college presidents were White, which

Table 3.1 Presidential Diversity: 2012 and 2016

| | | 2012 (%) | 2016 (%) |
|---|---|---|---|
| Age | 60–69 | 30 | 39 |
| | 50–59 | 52 | 38 |
| Gender | Male | 73.5 | 64 |
| | Female | 26.5 | 36 |
| Married or long-term partner | | 98 | 90 |
| Race/ethnicity | White | 80 | 80.2 |
| | Black/African-American | 6 | 7.9 |
| | Hispanic/Latinx | 3 | 3.8 |
| | Asian American/Pacific Islander | 1 | 2.3 |
| | Native-American/Alaska Native | 1 | 0.8 |
| | 2+ Races | 2 | 2.5 |
| | Other/Unknown | 7 | 3.2 |

Compiled from: AACC (2012, 2020), Howard and Gagliardi (2018), Jashik and Lederman (2018), Stripling (2017) and Tekle (2012).

changed to 80.2% in 2016. Nonetheless, it is revealing that in 2016, the combination of all Presidents of color was still only about 16% of all presidents, which meant that more than 80% were White (American College President Study, 2018). Even more troubling is that while some demographic changes were occurring at the staff level (AACC, 2020), they were not happening at the presidential level (Chen, 2017). Table 3.1 compares presidential profiles over time. Seltzer (2017) confirms that despite over a decade of talk about increasing diversity, community college presidents today look much like they did five years before – aging White men.

Finally, equitable gender representation for presidents is complicated. For the past 25 years, there has been notable growth in the percentage of women presidents (Eddy & Khwaja, 2019; Howard & Gagliardi, 2018; McKenney & Cejda, 2001; Philippe, 2020; Wiseman & Vaughan, 2002), and in 2016, women comprised 50% of all presidents (ACE, 2017). Nevertheless, in the past few years, there has been a slight decline in Latinx and women CEOs compared to just a few years ago (Jaschik & Lederman, 2018). These demographic patterns are similar to those found among mid-level administrative positions at community colleges (Stripling, 2019). In 2019, among all higher education presidents, only 33.9% were female (Chronicle of Higher Education, 2020). Finally, career pathways remain gendered, with 57% of men moving directly from a dean/vice-president position to the presidency compared to 18% of women (Stripling, 2017).

## RHETORIC VS. ACTION THAT DELAYS EQUITY IN LEADERSHIP

When viewing advocacy related to leaders approximating their constituencies, most of the nation's community colleges today are led by presidents who are mostly White males with an increasing number of presidents who are White females. It persists even though continued discussions on the need for diversity have been embedded in discussions on equity (Bell et al., 2018; Boggs, 2020; Gibson-Benninger et al., 1996). Massie (2016), in an article about affirmative action, quoted Kimberlé Crenshaw (2006) from the University of Michigan Law Review to demonstrate the continued inequities: "The primary beneficiaries of affirmative action have been Euro-American women and depicting a Black person as the poster child for affirmative action is flawed" (p. 3). Finley (2017) confirms that White women saw more growth in their careers in the first two decades of affirmative action than any racial group. Mahnken (2017) confirms that based on data from the National Center for Education Statistics, the share of White women in the role of President rose from 9.5% in 1986 to 30% in 2016.

It does not help the idea of advocacy that there are still those who disparage future Presidents of color. A 2017 survey of community college presidents conducted by Inside Higher Education and Gallup (Jaschik & Lederman, 2018) showed that community college presidents (mostly White) and other gatekeepers were pessimistic about the pool of qualified minority candidates for the top leadership position at community colleges. Oddly, they heartily agreed there are too few qualified minority candidates. In that same study, the report suggests just the opposite of potential White women leaders' quality. It is admittedly troublesome following decades of leadership training and outreach to future leaders of color to learn that there would be "few qualified" for the position. Beyond that, the survey says little about developmental strategies that could aid in eliminating this harmful stance.

Of noted concern is that there is a misalignment between the actual number of Presidents of color hired and outreach attempts. Job announcements model phrases such as "commitment to diversity," "interested in diversifying the faculty and staff," and "fairness and equal opportunity employer." This disconnect is worrisome and sad, given all the public rhetoric and policy development by national associations of higher education, public efforts by Boards, decision-making by CEOs with hiring authority, and millions of dollars spent on diversity training. Moreover, the needle has not significantly moved, and in too many cases, is regressing. Boards, executives, and faculty leaders will need to do a lot more than just list preferences and wish in job announcements to institute significant change.

## NEW DIRECTIONS

It is certain that leaders will retire and that the need to replace them will be ongoing. Decision-makers need a better comprehensive plan to select the next generation of presidents. In the American Association of Community Colleges (AACC) *Reclaiming America Report* (2012), Walter Bumphus, CEO of the American Association of Community Colleges opined that "we need to completely reimagine community colleges for today and the future" (p. 1). Similarly, Augie Gallego, Chancellor Emeritus, San Diego Community College District, and one of three cochair people (two being male and one female) of the above report, shared his vision with me:

> We must move now to reimagine the leadership to address those emerging controversial issues that face us in a new world order, evidence in the needs to address issues of economic, social, political and economic inequities, free speech, open carry, and #Me Too which are just a few of the challenges awaiting people who assume the role of president in our community colleges. (Phone interview, March 2018)

This revisioning is based on framing new questions to guide future discourse on identifying targets that should be set to show that leaders reflect the rising student populations of racial and ethnic minorities and ensure gender and sexual orientation equity. Finally, new strategies should be implemented to significantly improve presidents' hiring from nontraditional pathways, especially from younger leadership candidates.

In the future, those at universities who train new cohorts of future community college leaders, those sitting community college presidents who serve as mentors, and all stakeholders affiliated with community colleges need to take more substantial affirmative steps to achieve results grounded in equity. It could begin with seriously holding hiring committees and executive leaders accountable for achieving specified goals just as they do with budgets, student success, and program planning. It includes critically assessing whose vision has been perpetuated, and it is based on equity. Short of this action and monitoring the organization for achieving results, a decade from now, we are likely to be reading the same statistics reflecting too few racially and ethnically diverse presidents serving in leadership roles in community colleges nationwide.

## REFERENCES

American Association of Community Colleges (AACC). (2001). *Leadership 2020: Recruitment, preparation, and support*. ERIC ED493948.

American Association of Community Colleges (AACC). (2012). *Reclaiming the American dream*. www.aacc.nch.edu/AboutCC/21stcenturyreport/index.html.

American Association of Community Colleges (AACC). (2020). Fast facts. President profiles. www.aacc.nche.edu/research-trends/fast-facts/.

American Council on Education (ACE). (2017). Comprehensive demographic profile of American college presidents shows slow progress in diversifying leadership ranks. www.acenet.edu/news-room/Pages/Comprehensive-Demographic Profile-of-American-College-Presidents-Shows-Slow-Progress-in-Diversifying-Leadership-Ranks.aspx.

American Council on Education (ACE). (2019). Profile of American college presidents shows slow progress in diversifying leadership ranks. www.acenet.edu/news-room/Pages/Comprehensive-Demographic/aspx.

Bell, K., Donaghue, J., & Gordon, A. (2018). *Collaborative leadership: Advancing diversity, equity, and comprehensive internationalization in higher education*. Diversity Abroad White Paper.

Boggs, G. R. (2020). Roueche Center forum: Are we really serious about diversity, equity, and inclusion? https://diverseeducation.com/article/181549/pdf.

Chen, D. (2017). At colleges, demographic changes everywhere but the top. https://www.nytimes.com/2017/06/20/nyregion/college-president-survey-demographic-changes.html.

Chronicle of Higher Education. (2020). Chronicle of higher education 2020–2021 Almanac. Gender, race & ethnicity of noninstructional staff members, by employment status, Fall 2018: 2-year public institutions.

Eckel, P. D., Cook, B. J. & King, J. E. (2009). *The CAO census: A national profile of chief academic officers*. American Council on Education.

Eddy, P. L. (2009). Leading gracefully: Gendered leadership at community colleges. In *Women in academic leadership*. Edited by D.R. Dean, S.J. Bracken, & J.K. Allen (pp. 8–30). Stylus.

Eddy, P. L., & Khwaja, T. (2019). What happened to re-visioning community college leadership? A 25-year retrospective. *Community College Review*, 47(1), 53–78. doi:10.1177/0091552118818742.

Ellis, M. M., & Garcia, L. (2017). *Generation X presidents leading community colleges: New challenges, new leaders*. Rowan & Littlefield.

Finley, T. (2017). Affirmative action still matters. https://www.huffingtonpost.com/entry/affirmative-action-still-matters_us_5981d9b6e4b0353fbb33e1bb.

Gagliardi, J. S., Espinosa, L. L., Turk, J. M., & Taylor, M. (2017). *American college president study 2017*. American Council on Education.

Gallego, A. (2018). Chancellor Emeritus, San Diego Community College District. [Phone Interview, March 2018].

Gibson-Benninger, B. S., Ratliff, J. L., & Rhoads, R. A. (1996). Diversity, discourse, and democracy: Needed attributes in the next generation of community college leadership programs. *New Directions for Community Colleges*, 95, 65–75.

Howard, E., & Gagliardi, J. (2018). Leading the way to parity: Preparation, persistence, and the role of women presidents. ACE Center for Policy, Research, and Strategy (CPRS). www.acenet.edu/news-room/Pages/Leading-the-Way-to-Parity.aspx.

Jaschik, S., & Lederman, D. (2018). Survey of college and university presidents: A study by Inside Higher Ed and Gallup. Inside Higher Education. https://www.ellucian.com/assets/en/white-paper/whitepaper-2017-survey-community-college-presidents.pdf.

Mahnken, K. (2017). College presidents becoming more diverse but still mostly white men in their 60s. https://www.the74million.org/article/college-presidents.

Massie, V. M. (2016). White women benefit most from affirmative action – And are among its fiercest opponents. Vox.com, June 23, 2016. https://www.vox.com/2016/5/25/11682950/fisher-supreme-court-white-women-affirmative-action.

McFarlin, C. H., Crittenden, B. J., & Ebbers, L. H. (1999). Background factors common among outstanding community college presidents. *Community College Review*, 27(3), 19–31.

McKenney, C., & Cejda, B. (2001). The career path and profile of women chief academic officers in public community colleges. *Advancing Women in Leadership Journal.* http://www.advancingwomen.com/awl/summer2001/cejda_mckenney.html.

McNair, D. E. (2016). Deliberate disequilibrium: Preparing for a community college presidency. *Community College Review*, 43(1), 72–88.

Philippe, K. (2020). AACC DataPoints: Faculty and staff diversity. June 6, 2018. https://www.aacc.nche.edu/2018/06/06/datapoints-faculty-and-staff-diversity/.

Piland, W. E., & Wolf, D. B. (2003). *Help wanted: Preparing community college leaders in a new century.* Jossey-Bass.

Prator, R. (1963). *The college president.* Center for Applied Research in Education, Inc.

Seltzer, R. (2017). College presidents diversifying slowly and growing older. *Inside Higher Education.* https://www.insidehighered.com/news/2017/06/20/college-presidents-diversifying-slowly-and-growing-older-study-finds.

Shults, C. (2001). *The critical impact of impending retirements on community college leadership.* Research Brief Leadership Series, no. 1 RB-01-5. American Association of Community Colleges.

Stripling, J. (2017). The profession. Characteristics of college presidents. *Chronicle of Higher Education*, August 18, 24–28.

Stripling, J. (2019). Behind a stagnant portrait of the presidency. *Chronicle of Higher Education*. https://www.chronicle.com/article/Behind-a-Stagnant-Portrait-of/240393.

Tekle, R. (2012). *Compensation and benefits of community college CEOs*. American Association of Community Colleges Research Brief. http://www.aacc.nche.edu/AboutCC/Trends/Documents/CEOCompensation-ResearchBrief.pdf.

Thwing, C. F. (1926). *The college president*. MacMillan.

Vaughan, G. B. (1989). *Leadership in transition: The community college presidency*. American Association of Community Colleges.

Weltsch, M. D. (2009). A study of community college presidential qualifications and career paths. [Unpublished Doctoral Dissertation] Kansas State University.

Wheelhouse: The Center for Community College Leadership and Research. (2016). Tough job if you can keep it: What California community college CEOs say about their challenges and longevity. *Research Brief*, 1(1). http://education.ucdavis.edu/sites/main/files/ucdavis_wheelhouse_tough_job_research_brief.pdf.

Wiseman, I. M. & Vaughan, G. B. (1998). *The community college presidency at the millennium*. American Association of Community Colleges.

Wiseman, I. M. & Vaughan, G. B. (2002). *The community college presidency, 2001*. (Report No. AACC-RB-02-1; AACC Ser-3). American Association of Community Colleges.

Wiseman, I. M. & Vaughan, G. B. (2007). The community college presidency: 2006. http://www.aacc.nche.edu/Publications/Briefs/Documents/09142007-presidentbrief.pdf.

Chapter Four

# Multiple Generations of Community College Leadership Revisited

Since 1940, the community college presidency's role and power have changed with the times. This chapter is informed by Tillery and Deegan's (1985) history of the community college construct, Sullivan's (2001) categorization of generational development, and Boggs and McPhail's (2016) leadership paradigms. In this chapter, I present the different generations of new community college leaders' characterizations and examine the changing context of the leadership position's purpose. Table 4.1 summarizes the changing duties and philosophies over time.

## FIRST GENERATION (1940–1960)

The first Generation of new community college presidents were White married men in their 50s who rose through the academic ranks. The significance of being married was that it afforded the men time to devote long hours to the college as their wives ran their homes for them (Eddy & Khwaja, 2020). Sullivan (2001) refers to these individuals as "founding fathers." Some of these presidents had military experience that included service in World War II and the Korean War. Their styles were based on a combination of secondary school leadership, university leadership, and military leadership traits. Many also had experience working within a hierarchical organizational structure within the American industry's existing business model at that time. Identified as founders and builders, they acted as powerful gatekeepers of their organization with unofficial power over who got promoted or let in and were supported by a finely

Table 4.1 Changing Focus of Duties and Philosophies over Time

| | Pre-1960 | 1970–1985 | 1985–1990 | 1990–2010 | 2010–2020 |
|---|---|---|---|---|---|
| Duties | Conduct faculty meetings<br>Visit classes<br>Promote interests of college<br>Articulate aims of the college<br>Secure buy-in of others<br>Set tone of the institution<br>Enable staff to achieve goals<br>Support academic freedom<br>Be an ex-officio member of the Board of Trustees<br>Do duties conferred to by Board of Trustees<br>Be good manager | Redefine mission<br>Support organizational behavior<br>Support quality improvement<br>Encourage team-building<br>Explore multiple leadership styles | Reject traditional decision-making<br>Use existing resources within limited state funding | Use participatory governance model<br>Represent college interests to the community<br>Sign legal documents, contracts, and diplomas<br>Know technology skills | Exercise leadership<br>Be bold and courageous<br>Be risk-averse |
| Philosophy | Superintending<br>Facilitating<br>Developing<br>Leading | Collaborators | Manage | Learning-Centered | Change Agent |

Compiled from: Boggs and McPhail (2016), Mitchell and Eddy (2008), O'Banion (2019), Sullivan (2001), Tillery and Deegan (1985), Sullivan (2001).

tuned network. This Generation developed the new community colleges as a unique entity and whose mission was directed with core values and practices that exist today (Roueche, 1989; Vickers 2007). Like today, these presidents had to lead with small budgets, but they had the absolute authority to be creative (Sullivan, 2001). In this period, the community college's purpose is best described as creating a new context for high school graduates' transitioning to postsecondary education and the world of work.

## SECOND GENERATION (1960–1970)

The Second Generation of community college presidents was also White men who were married and identified as good managers (Sullivan, 2001). Many had the first-generation presidents as their mentors and adopted similar leadership styles. One deviation was the embrace of industrial concepts of collective bargaining and the university model of faculty relations. In the late 1960s, these presidents experienced the civil rights movement, the anti-Vietnam War movement, and the women's rights movement. Vaughan (1986) writes that these presidents saw and promoted the concept of "open access" and fostered a strong belief in the merits of higher education because of this experience. They referred to the community college as "the people's college." New discussions began on patriarchal models' embracing practices that stem from leading based on authority, which was beginning to be recognized as different from women's leadership styles and leaders of color who favored more collaborative leadership styles (Sullivan, 2001). Under these leaders, the small community college system grew into large bureaucracies with large physical plants, extensive resources, and robust community support via levied taxes. Within this context, the power of the presidency grew.

## THIRD GENERATION (1970–1985)

Sullivan (2001) labeled the third generation of community college presidents as the collaborators. Most of these leaders came from middle-class families that instilled the value of education as a means of moving upward in society, which in turn shaped their professional lives. Many were the first in their family to go to college, and they believed in the opportunities that higher education could bring. It was the first generation in which most majored in education, social sciences, or the humanities. Due to their past experiences, many championed the expansion of higher education to traditionally disenfranchised groups, making opportunities to participate equitable and accessible. Unlike the previous two generations, this generation of presidents intentionally prepared themselves for the community college presidency. They did so via their graduate degree choices in higher education administration and leadership experiences and prepared themselves through professional development programs specific to community college leadership. These leaders were knowledgeable in organizational behavior, change processes, and quality improvement, and they believed in the team-building concept. Being taught by the last generation of leadership, they adopted considerable skills in moving through different frames and leadership style (Moore et al., 1985; Vaughan, 1989). That said, Sullivan (2001) suggests that women and leaders of color felt excluded from the traditional power structure that favored a distinctive leadership style seen as White Male focused. In response, new leadership traits emerged that included elements of anti-structure, anti-authority, and anti-oppression.

## FOURTH GENERATION (1985–1990)

The fourth Generation of community college presidents marked a shift in how leadership was conceived. It is called Preparation Generation that helped to build what Boggs and McPhail (2019) call the Contemporary Community College. While discussions on the need for affirmative action expanded, the rhetoric was louder than the results. Presidential demographics remained similar to previous generations being dominated by married White men. However, based on the previous Generation of leadership's voices, a small emerging cast of women, racial, and ethnic minorities started to change the field, bringing their unique leadership styles. The presidents in this Generation were born after the world wars, the civil rights movements of the 1960s, and the economic crises of the late 1970s. Most were greatly influenced by the emerging technologies of computers and the internet that were beginning to change how leaders needed to conduct daily business. Unlike the previous Generation, they had more of a focus on workforce development than social justice. This Generation had intentionally trained for the presidency and appeared to be more sophisticated and knowledgeable than their predecessors when stepping into the presidency (Birnbaum, 1988). Despite being trained by the third-generation leaders, this Generation of presidents critiqued traditionally prescribed decision-making processes and the directed policymaking standard procedures in the Third Generation (Duncan & Harlacher, 1991). In turn, they adopted a new leadership construct that focused on finding as many possibilities for a solution as possible, including bringing in new voices to the leadership process. In an attempt to meet the "open doors" philosophy, new educational programs were designed at the community college to reach new groups of students that included noncredit offerings, fee-based courses, community services programs, and expanded occupational and technical education program offerings. Simultaneously, government funding for higher education decreased substantially and was complicated by tax revolts creating formulas to guarantee even less funding. Consequently, there was an essential focus on managing and using existing resources within limited state funding. In this period, stress points for the community college related to supporting open-door policies, serving diverse populations, and responding to legislative mandates without the needed resources to implement them.

## FIFTH GENERATION (1990–2010)

The fifth Generation of community college presidents, coined by Sullivan (2001) as the Millennium Generation, saw a significant change in the demographics due to the increasing number of White women in the presidents' roles (Mitchell & Eddy, 2008). Taken together, nonwhite racial and ethnic groups also experienced slight gains, but not in proportion to the diverse makeup of the student populations (Kubala & Bailey, 2001; Wiseman & Vaughan, 2007). The training of presidents and the teaching of leadership competencies became a focus of this Generation due to the high number of Sitting Presidents who were retiring (Campbell & Leverty, 1997; Vaughan, 2006). Future leaders became more conscious of the need for training beyond their academic achievements and professional experiences. The voices in leadership training were filled by the American Association of Community Colleges (AACC) and university Educational Leadership doctoral programs. In particular, the AACC created a series of frameworks that outlined leadership competencies (AACC, 2005, 2020) that were taught by Sitting Presidents, which were accepted by all. The importance of the older generation teaching the newer Generation shows continuity in leadership styles. For example, the AACC leadership training programs specifically taught competencies to formalize personal and professional skills deemed necessary for future leaders to know (Cain, 1999; Cohen & Kisker, 2010).

New shifts in what was considered appropriate skill sets began with what Boggs and McPhail (2019) claimed was a learning-centered era, where a significant shift was made from learning processes to learning results. Emphasis was increasingly placed on the importance of research and data analysis skills and the ability to align those results to ground future reform efforts. Some scholars note that the participatory style competencies that were beginning to be integrated into the leadership style in this era mirrored more feminine leadership styles, including an emphasis on collaboration, shared communication, and service to others (Eddy & Khwaja, 2020).

## SIXTH GENERATION (2010–2020)

As part of the Millennial Generation, these presidents are greatly influenced by the political terrorism of 9/11, the economic crises of the Great Recession of 2008, and the country's political polarization. Many are also being influenced by social issues of systemic racism and inequity (Pew, 2020), as society approaches the third decade of 2020. They are beginning discussions to refocus the community college mission for social justice, including equity issues fueled by measurable change. They are pressed on social and political issues facing their colleges, including food and home insecurity, educational and economic inequities, #Me Too, Black Lives Matter, All Lives Matter, the right to carry laws, immigration, and LGBTQ+ rights and more recently Covid 19. Finally, leaders in this Generation are increasingly embracing international education as an agenda to create global learning-centered villages that have a culture of student exchange, study abroad, and collaborative faculty teaching. These college presidents view themselves as global learners and increasingly serve as goodwill ambassadors for community colleges' internalization worldwide (Raby & Valeau, 2016).

Two leadership styles were emphasized in the 2010s. The first leadership style is that of the transformational leader who can turn personal vision into facilitated action (AACC, 2013; Astin & Astin, 2000). Included in this process is a change-agent leader (Boggs & McPhail, 2016), who has a vision and is intentional in using that vision to guide action (Mathis & Roueche, 2013; McNair et al., 2011). It is a leader who inspires others to buy- into their vision to collectively work for change (AACC, 2015) with the intent to create systematic change. The more senior the position, the more expectation there is to create and sustain innovations (O'Banion, 2019), making directed leadership all the more important. Simultaneously, due to the increase in women presidents, new feminine leadership styles are emerging and focus on participatory leadership styles (Eddy & Khwaja, 2019). However, in the era of accountability, the feminine leadership styles are less valued, while more masculine images of power to manage and lead are becoming the vision forward.

The other leadership style is that of entrepreneurialism. The entrepreneurial creator begins with a vision grounded in identifying an opportunity to build something that did not previously exist (AACC, 2020). In this context, the identified resources are not just money but are also relationships, networks, and knowledge. There is an intentionality to create something based on a specific need and for others to strategically revision alternatives during the implementation stage. The leader then conducts outreach to influence a range of college stakeholders to get buy-in for that vision. The "thinking out-of-the-box" and pioneering mentality allows leaders to look differently at problems than to try things that others have not. In sum, they use their ability to think two steps ahead to mitigate potential problems (O'Banion, 2019). In this context, the field visibly and ceremoniously rewards leaders who are courageous, bold, and risk-averse (AACC, 2020; O'Banion, 2019). Finally, during this current Generation, more than ever, the role of the presidency has become one that is more highly respected, valued, and supported as an acceptable change agent in the field of higher education (Boggs, 2004; Mathis & Roueche, 2013).

## SEVENTH GENERATION (2020–2040)

The most recent generation of community college presidents is currently being shaped. In terms of demographics, this is the Generation of notable change with more diverse leaders influenced by White women, women and men of color, and gays who gain more significant numbers in leadership roles. Many of these leaders bring new leadership styles in which they decompartmentalize Generation X's generational values and norms while integrating new norms for today (Ellis & Garcia, 2017). Two very different generations of presidents will emerge in the ending decade of the 2020s and early years of the 2040s. The first is the Millennial President's maturity (Ashford, 2019), while the second is the Generation Z president. People born between 1981 and 1996 are seen as Millennials, while those born after 1997 are seen as Generation Z. In 2000, the oldest Millennials were 39 years old, while the youngest Generation Z are 23 years old.

The youngest Millennials presidents and senior administrators in pathways for the presidency are influenced by how they were raised. They are mostly the children of the Baby Boomers and the technology age and are now in their maturation related to career building. They often identify as a race or ethnicity that is something other than non-Hispanic Whites. They are technology-savvy, often the first in their family to attend college, and are results-driven with a sense of "let us get it done." They are also highly college educated (Fry & Parker, 2018), and have surpassed the Baby Boomers as the nation's largest living adult generation.

Many are part of a "slow starts" context, in which they choose to delay their life and job choices. Some Millennials are entering the presidency younger (35–45), and unlike previous generations, some have a more enlightened view of society mostly fueled by the rapid expansion of knowledge and access to technology to manage it and expand their learning. They are influenced by the youth vote of the 2008 election. Finally, they entered the workforce after the Great Recession in a time of austerity. Through their experience as students in the system, their leadership pipeline is professionals in unrelated fields, adjunct faculty, college coordinators, assistant deans, and deans rising through the ranks, not unlike the previous Generation.

The Generation Z presidents have not yet assumed their positions, but will soon be entering the leadership pipelines and future presidents. Generation Z were born after 1997 and grew up in the late 2000s and early 2010s. Though in their teens for President Obama's 2008 election, more were influenced by President Trump's 2016 election. While some experienced the 2008 economic crisis and years of austerity, most came of age in the recovery years of economic stability and advancement. Generation

Z experienced the interruption of their education and their professional lives due to COVID-19 pandemic. A recent survey shows that friends who are already working were influenced by friends who have died, lost their jobs, and took pay decreases because of COVID. Those in college and high school had disrupted educational experiences that will undoubtedly influence them as adults.

Generation Z are more racially and ethnically diverse than the Millennials, and as such, Generation Z presidents will likely be the most racially and ethnically diverse, including more female and LGBTQI+ presidents. Their generational ties should easily facilitate their engagement with students of all demographic backgrounds. Significantly, most are children of immigrants, and many are First Generation in college. Nevertheless, 44% of Generation Z have parents who have earned a BA degree (Pew, 2020). Generation Z are predicted to be the most well educated of all living generations.

In surveys of Generation Z (Pew, 2020), the vast majority outwardly support progressive policies, including understanding the consequences of Climate Change, supporting and participating in #BlacklivesMatter protests, and leaning toward using gender-neutral pronouns. This Generation is the social media generation and does not know a time without the smartphone. Online gaming and social media trends, such as Tick-Tock, WhatsApp, Zoom, and Instagram, are their wheelhouses and provide a global sense of community. Generation Z attend events that Millennials' presidents would not be comfortable in attending. Therefore, future leaders might be more in touch with their students and their interests.

In terms of predicted presidential traits, due to the age and experiences in which Generation Z were raised, they likely have a strong penchant for being inclusive as an intentional organizational strategy. It is also likely that they will not accept age as a defining point of their preparation and readiness for the job, but will point to their record of accomplishments systematically gaining breadth and depth of experience leading them to the presidency, even if they are significantly younger than their predecessors. In this context, they more readily accept the hard educational work needed to become a community college president in an evolving and changing educational environment. They are intentionally aware of issues like inadequate financing, shifting demographics, political polarization, pandemics, and the positive and negative impacts of technology on education. They will be better prepared with current innovations and strategies to meet the challenges of the day. As such, these future presidents will not be one-dimensional, but will be adept at responding rather than reacting to change while acknowledging institutional shortcomings.

Finally, their leadership style will be influenced by the leadership of the 2020s that focuses on leaders who are transformative, who embrace risk, and who manage change effectively with data. However, they will tend toward being risk-averse. Their leadership responses will be rapid because of how they prepare themselves and later their colleges to use data for decision-making (Vogles, 2019). Specifically, they will know how to mine data for effective communication, decision-making aimed at staff, and institutional effectiveness. They will also be receptive to executive coaching provided by progressive boards and current leaders who set the tone for a leadership change. Their training will focus on the strengths of being collaborative leaders with a high degree of transparency, thus lessening faculty resistance to their leadership. Significantly, they will be more apt to engage in participatory governance, seeing it as a strength rather than a "to do." As younger staff members, they will be aware of the need to look for mentors to teach them how to be transparent, decisive, committed, and understand the values of faculty, staff, students, and community. Because of their predecessors' mentoring and coaching and accepting of their wisdom, millennial presidents will embrace old and true guides to effective leadership, as discussed throughout this book. For this book, and based on the above discussion, these presidents are referred to as the Enlightened Generation.

## REFERENCES

American Association of Community Colleges (AACC). (2005). *Competency framework for community college leaders.* http://www.aacc.nche.edu/competency_framework/pdf.

American Association of Community Colleges (AACC). (2013). *Competencies for community college leaders.* Second Edition. AACC. www.aacc.nche.edu/newsevents/Events/leadershipsuite/Documents/ AACC/Core Competencies/web.pdf.

American Association of Community Colleges (AACC). (2015). Emerging Leaders. Leadership institute documents. www.aacc.nche.edu/newsevents/Emergingleaders/leadershipsuiteDocuments/AACC.

American Association of Community Colleges (AACC). (2020). *Competencies for community college leaders.* Third Edition. www.aacc.nche.edu/publications-news/aacc-competencies-for-community-college-leaders/.

Ashford, E. (2019). The newest generations of Presidents. *Community College Daily.* https://www.ccdaily.com/2019/07/newest-generation-presidents/org.

Astin, A. W., & Astin, H. S. (2000). *Leadership reconsidered: Engaging higher education in social change.* W.K. Kellogg Foundation. http://eric.ed.gov/?id=ED444437.

Birnbaum, R. (1988). *How colleges work: The cybernetics of academic organization and leadership.* Jossey-Bass.

Boggs, G. R. (2004). The leader as an agent of change and stability. Paper presentation: The American Association of Community Colleges Future Leader Institute in Long Beach, California [July].

Boggs, G. R., & McPhail, C. J. (2016). *Practical leadership in community colleges: Navigating today's challenges.* John Wiley and Sons/Jossey-Bass.

Boggs, G. R., & McPhail, C. J. (2019). *Team leadership in community colleges.* Jossey-Bass.

Cain, M. S. (1999). *The community college in the twenty-first century: A system approach.* University Press of America.

Campbell, D. F., & Leverty, L. H. (1997). Developing and selecting leaders for the 21st century. *Community College Journal*, 67, 34–36.

Cohen, A. M., & Kisker, C. B. (2010). *American higher education: Emergence and growth of the contemporary system.* Second Edition. Wiley.

Duncan, A. H., & Harlacher, E. L. (1991). The twenty-first-century executive leader. *Community College Review*, 18(4), 39–47.

Eddy, P. L., & Khwaja, T. (2019). What happened to re-visioning community college leadership? A 25-year retrospective. *Community College Review*, 47(1), 53–78. doi:10.1177/0091552118818742.

Ellis, M. M. & Garcia, L. (2017). *Generation X presidents leading community colleges: New challenges, new leaders.* Rowan & Littlefield.

Fry, R., & Parker, K. (2018). Millennials overtake baby boomers as America's largest generation. *Pew Research.* https://www.pewsocialtrends.org/2018/11/15/early-benchmarks-show-post-millennials-on-track-to-be-most-diverse-best-educated-generation-yet/.

Kubala, T. S. & Bailey, G. M. (2001). A new perspective on community college presidents: Results of a national study. *Community College Journal of Research and Practice*, 25, 793–804.

Mathis, M. B., & Roueche, J. E. (2013, June 24). POV: Preparation of future leaders takes on new urgency. *Community College Week.* www.ccweek.com.

Mitchell, R. L. G., & Eddy, P. L. (2008). In the middle: Career pathways of midlevel community college leaders. *Community College Journal of Research and Practice*, 32(10), 793–811. https://doi.org/10.1080/10668920802325739.

McNair, D. E., Duree, C. A., & Ebbers, L. (2011). If I knew then what I know now: Using the leadership competencies developed by the American Association of Community Colleges to prepare community college presidents. *Community College Review*, 39(1), 3–25.

Moore, K., Martorana, S., & Twombly, S. (1985). *Today's academic leaders: A national study of administrators in two-year colleges.* Center for the Study of Higher Education.

O'Banion, T. (2019). *13 Ideas that are transforming the community college world*. Rowman and Littlefield.

Pew Research Center. (2020). On the cusp of adulthood and facing an uncertain future. What we know about Generation Z so far. https://www.pewsocialtrends.org/essay/on-the-cusp-of-adulthood-and-facing-an- uncertain-future-what-we-know-about-gen-z-so-far

Raby, R. L., & Valeau, E. J. (2016). *International education at community colleges: Themes, practices, research, and case studies*. Palgrave Publishers.

Roueche, J. (1989). *Shared vision: Transformational leadership in American community colleges*. American Association of Community Colleges Press.

Sullivan, L. G. (2001). Four generations of community college leadership. *Community College Journal of Research and Practice*, 25(4), 559–571. doi:10.1080/106689201316880759.

Tillery, D., & Deegan, W. (1985). The evolution of two-year colleges through four generations. In *Renewing the American community college: Priorities and strategies for effective leadership*. Edited by D. Deegan, & D. Tillery. Jossey-Bass.

Vaughan, G. B. (1986). *The Community college presidency*. American Council on Education/Macmillan.

Vaughan, G. B. (1989). *Leadership in transition: The community college presidency*. American Association of Community Colleges.

Vaughan, G. B. (2006). *The community college story: A tale of American innovation*. AACC/National Center for Higher Education.

Vickers, K. J. (2007). An assessment of leadership development programs for employees in Iowa community colleges. [Unpublished Doctoral Dissertation]. Iowa State University.

Vogles, E. A. (2019). Millennials stand out for their technology use, but older generations also embrace digital life. https://www.pewresearch.org/fact-tank/2019/09/09/us-generations-technology-use/org.

Wiseman, I. M. & Vaughan, G. B. (2007). The community college presidency: 2006. http://www.aacc.nche.edu/Publications/Briefs/Documents/09142007-presidentbrief.pdf.

Chapter Five

# Student and Faculty Profiles

The community college's marketization gained great impetus in 1946 with President Truman's Commission on Higher Education publication of *Higher Education for American Democracy* (Zook, 1947). It established a network of public community colleges, often referred to as *People's Colleges*. They were to charge little or no tuition, serve as cultural centers, be comprehensive in program offerings with an emphasis on civic responsibilities, and serve the area in which they were located. It transformed the community college movement into a different form of a noble deed, one that linked higher education to a form of democracy. The community college's role stood in direct opposition to the more elitist university models where only the privileged were thought to be worthy of and could receive the benefits of higher education. The foundation of the philosophy of open access had a goal of the massification of higher education by institutions other than the university (Raby & Valeau, 2009). It resulted in expanding access to higher education to new student populations (Cohen et al., 2014). Over time, without question, community colleges have been able to carry out a crucial function in higher education by providing college access, including baccalaureate opportunities, occupational education, remedial and developmental education, and other educational services (Dougherty et al., 2017).

While access was a hallmark of the community college, actual enrollment opportunities were highly stratified along with socioeconomic status and racial categorizations (Cohen, 1974). Although the principal of open access allowed widespread admission, not all students had equitable experiences (Karabel, 1972). The community college itself supported a hidden agenda that purposefully lead individual students (blue-collar types, minorities, immigrants, and women) away from attending academic classes that could prepare them for transfer to the university. There was a belief that if these students attended an elite university (Jencks & Riesman, 1968), they would be a burden and eventually bring down academic standards.

Within the community college, differential access was done through a "cooling out" (Clark, 1968) process in which students were tracked with the underlying assumption that only some would succeed. The tracking placed some students in a transfer pathway, while many more were not. Today, stratification continues with the vocationalization of the institution (Jencks & Riesman, 1968), the negative impacts of remedial education (Irwin & Oakley, 2018), the inequitable access to emerging technologies (Hu, 2020), and the continued racial, ethnic, and gender inequities that influence persistence and completion (O'Banion, 2019). Since there is a known link between educational participation and improved career benefits and societal benefits resulting from an educated citizenry, these inequities remain of deep concern for the future and will continue to be a stain on community colleges.

## STUDENT PROFILES

Community colleges are a primary gateway to postsecondary education, especially for graduates from low socioeconomic high schools. American Association of Community Colleges (AACC) data (2020a) shows that community colleges educate more than 12 million students each year. Of the students pursuing higher education in the United States, roughly 40% of first-year students start in community colleges (Shapiro et al., 2016). Among students who started postsecondary education at two-year public institutions, 42% are from low-income families (Pew Research, 2019). Nonetheless, Page and Scott-Clayton (2015) suggest that college enrollment's socioeconomic gaps have widened over time, despite increasing returns to postsecondary education. In addition, even with significant policy efforts to improve access to the university, community college transfers are still a concern.

The average age of a community college student is 27. As adult learners (Van Noy & Zeidenberg, 2017), they are motivated to learn and take advantage of all college programs and offerings. In 2020, 29% of students were first generation, 15% were single parents, 9% were non-US citizens, 5% were veterans, 20% were students with disabilities, and 8% were students with prior bachelor's degree (AACC, 2020a). Nationwide, the student population is diverse with 41% White, 24% Hispanic/Latinx, 13% African-Americans, 6% Asian/Pacific Islander, 3% two or more races,

1% Native-American 1%, 4% other/unknown, and 2% nonresident alien. From 1996 to 2016, the percentage of students of color increased from 29.6% to 45.2%. It was driven by an almost doubling of the percentage of Latinx students (AACC, 2020b).

## STUDENT PERSISTENT AND RETENTION RATES

In the past decade, there has been a concerted focus on persistence and retention, with much of it tied to Performance-Based Funding policies (Tandberg et al., 2014). The persistence rate is the percentage of students who continue their postsecondary education at any institution for their second year. In contrast, the retention rate is the percentage of students who return to the same institution.

Persistence rates are higher than retention rates for community college students. For students who started college at two-year public institutions in fall 2017, the persistence rate was 62.3% (National Student Clearinghouse Research Center (NCES), 2019). While up 1.3% from the fall 2009 cohort, still one year after entering community college, six out of ten students had either enrolled at the original institution (retained), transferred to a different four- or two-year institution (persisted), or completed a postsecondary degree or certificate. Full-time students have more remarkable persistence at 69.7% compared to 56.3% for part-time students. Additionally, persistence rates differ among different racial and ethnic groups. Of students who started in fall 2017, persistence rates were 71% for Asian students, 67.1% for White students, and 42% for Black/African-American students (NCES, 2019). Persistence accounting has been criticized as not all community college students are continuous enrollees, and those who stop-out for a time, returning years later, are not included in data collection (Fink & Jenkins, 2020). Notably, there are also inconsistencies in the Federal Integrated Postsecondary Education Data System (IPEDS) that counts only first-time, full-time students. It then automatically reclassifies public two-year institutions that offer Baccalaureate degrees as public four-year institutions (Fink & Jenkins, 2020) and show a preference for degree-granting student profiles (Barringer & Jaquette, 2018).

About two-thirds of community college students leave their programs after having completed a year or less coursework over five years. Schneider and Yin (2012) warn about the high cost of low graduation rates as a contributing factor to economic and societal inequities. Deficit based reasons for the lack of persistence include the fact that many students have an unequal K-12 educational experience that is believed to impede educational progress and success (Adelman, 2006), making these students not ready to succeed. Anti-deficit reasons examine the constraints of remedial education (Irwin & Oakley, 2018), systemic racism (Long, 2016), and that some students choose to use the college to work pipeline (Wang, 2013). Finally, new student success initiatives (O'Banion, 2019) improve academic standing for the least prepared.

Future issues for serving students need to focus on open access and understand that existing inequities disadvantage various student groups. Pfeffer and Goldrick-Rab (2014) talk about the need to attend to heterogeneity. Thus, there needs to be a focus on how cost and debt are linked to a lack of completion (Goldrick-Rab et al., 2016) and persistence regarding who stays in (Castelman & Long, 2016).

## STUDENT TRANSFERS

New measures of calculating transfer now focus on the community college's unique profiles and its student populations. For example, the transfer-out rate is calculated by dividing the number of students who transferred out of the community college to a four-year institution by the number of students in the college's entering cohort. Using this formula, Shapiro et al. (2016) examine students' average transfer-out rate in the fall 2010 cohort. They found that community colleges award proportionally more occupational credentials and more academic degrees. Both had similar transfer-out rates (33.2% vs. 29.9%, respectively). Colleges located in suburbs or towns had a slightly higher transfer-out rate on average (32.4%) than those in urban and rural locations (30.8% and 30.5%, respectively). Expectedly, community colleges that serve wealthier students had higher transfer-out rates than those serving lower socioeconomic status (SES) students. The average transfer-out rate among colleges, whose median student SES was in the top quintile, was 8% higher than that of the community colleges that serve higher proportions of lower SES students (34.6% and 26.3%, respectively). This study also found that 36.1% of transfer students from primarily academic and 31.1% of those from primarily occupational programs earned a certificate or associate degree before transferring to four-year institutions. Transfer students from rural (34.3%) and suburban/town (34.9%) community college locations were more likely to transfer after earning a certificate or associate degree than students from urban (32.4%) locations. Community colleges that serve students in the top socioeconomic quintiles had higher transfer-with-award rates than community colleges that serve students in the low socioeconomic quintiles (35.1% and 31.7%, respectively).

## STUDENT CERTIFICATE AND DEGREE COMPLETION

Today, the VFA metrics are considered a better measure of community college student success than traditional IPEDS metrics. VFA measures all entering students and shows that 59% show completion within six years. Completion is measured along with nine different outcomes. IPEDS shows that 25% of students complete and measure only the first-time, full-time students and look at them only within three years to complete and only those who graduate (AACC, 2020c).

Lichtenberger and Dietrich (2017) found that while community college attendance can extend the time to degree, it has little bearing on bachelor's degree completion after six years of enrollment. Jenkins and Fink (2016) revealed that lower-income students were as likely as higher-income students to earn an associate degree or certificate before transferring to four-year institutions, but less likely to transfer or earn a bachelor's degree after transfer. Other studies show that although most students transfer from community colleges without a degree (Shapiro, 2016), the likelihood they will earn a bachelor's degree from a four-year institution is more significant if they earned a certificate or an associate degree before transferring. In this study, 13.3% of students who started at a community college completed a bachelor's degree at any four-year institution within six years. The bachelor's completion rate of students who started at community colleges with primarily an academic focus was higher than those who started at institutions with a primarily occupational focus (14.9% vs. 11.7%) (Shapiro, 2016). Bachelor's completion rates at suburban community colleges were higher (14.1%) than those who were enrolled in rural (12.7%) and urban (12.6%) community colleges. Like the community colleges' average transfer-out rate results, the cohort completion rates were higher (15.5%) for students who transferred from community colleges that serve predominately higher SES students than institutions that primarily serve students from lower SES backgrounds (9.4%).

Finally, Belfield and Bailey (2017) show higher earnings for community college awardees, and on average, community college students earn significantly more over their lifetimes than individuals who do not go to community college. Based on a large-scale study from six states, the average student who completes an associate degree at a community college will earn $5,400 more each working year than a student who drops out of community college. Certificates provide higher earnings as well and advantage those in health fields and technology. Finally, certificates increase the probability that the person is employed and that the job is in an industry related to their skills (Xu & Trimble, 2015).

## FACULTY AND STAFF PROFILES

The faculty's racial and ethnic profile does not parallel that of the student body enrolled, but the profiles of noninstructional staff numbers are approaching equity. In 2018, 73% of staff in management, 63% in student services, and 75% of faculty were White (AACC, 2020d). In 2019, community college staff saw a significant change in diversity with noninstructional staff as 65.1% White and 34.9% of those of color. In 2019, noninstructional staff at community colleges had the following representation: 1.0% American-Indian/Alaskan Native; 3.8% Asian; 15.3% Black; 13.1% Latino; 0.3% Native Hawaiian Pacific Islander; 65.1% White; 1.3% 2+ races; and 2.6% race unknown. Also, 61.6% of these staff members were women (Chronicle of Higher Education, 2020).

The diversity of faculty depends on the faculty rank. Table 5.1 shows the faculty diversity changes when comparing profiles from 2002 and 2016, in which faculty of color only grew from 15.1% to 20%. Racial inequalities also exist between different types of faculty ranks. Seventy-seven percent of full-time faculty are White compared to 74% of part-time faculty. A larger share of White (15.1%) compared to Native Hawaiian/other Pacific Islanders (14.9%) were full-time faculty. More faculty at the instructor, lecturer, and faculty with no academic rank were American-Indian or Alaska Native (76.3%), Native Hawaiian/Pacific Islander (54.2%), and International faculty (52.8%). Figure 5.1 shows the range of diversity of selected staff by race/ethnicity, according to the AACC (2020d).

Table 5.1 Racial Comparisons of Faculty: Comparing 2002 and 2016

| Full-Time Faculty | 2002 (%) | 2016 (%) |
|---|---|---|
| White | 83 | 76.8 |
| African-American | 6.3 | 7.4 |
| Hispanic/Latinx | 4.5 | 6.7 |
| Asian | 3.5 | 4.2 |
| Native-American/Alaskan Native | 0.8 | 0.08 |
| Native Hawaiian/Other Pacific Islander | NA | 0.02 |
| International | 0.5 | 0.7 |
| Two or more races | NA | 0.9 |
| Unknown | 0.5 | 2.2 |

Compiled from AACC (2020d), Philippe and Sullivan (2002).

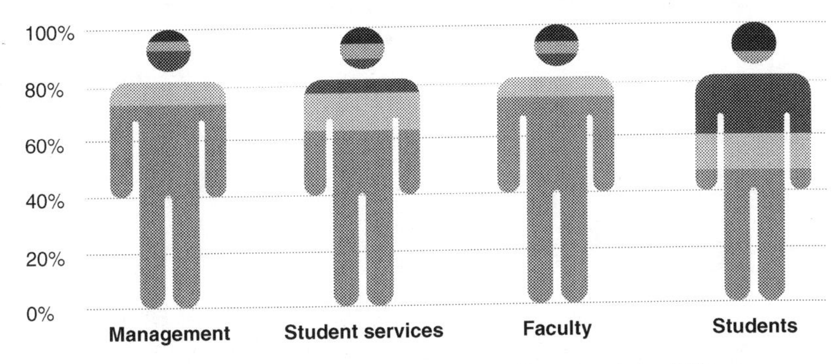


Figure 5.1 AACC Datapoints: Faculty and Staff Diversity: 6/6/2018.

## REFERENCES

Adelman, C. (2006). *The toolbox revisited: Paths to degree completion from high school through college.* US Department of Education. ERIC. ED490195.

American Association of Community Colleges (AACC).

(2020a). Fast facts. Students. www.aacc.nche.edu/research-trends/fast-facts.

(2020b). Fast facts. Race and ethnicity diversity of students. www.aacc.nche.edu/research-trends/fast-facts.

(2020c). Fast facts. Student completion rates. www.aacc.nche.edu/research-completion/fast-facts.

(2020d). Fast facts. Faculty diversity. www.aacc.nche.edu/research-trends/fast-facts/.

Documents/CC%20Presidency%20Meeting%202012-13.pdf.

Barringer, S. N., & Jaquette, O. (2018). The moving missions of community colleges: An examination of degree-granting profiles over time. *Community College Review*, 46(12). Online First. doi:10.1177/0091552118786012.

Belfield, C. R., & Bailey, T. (2017). The labor market returns to sub-baccalaureate college: A review. Center for Analysis of Postsecondary Education and Employment (CAPSEE) Working Paper. https://ccrc.tc.columbia.edu/media/k2/attachments/labor-market-returns-sub-baccalaureate-college-review.pdf.

Castelman, B. L., & Long, B. T. (2016). Looking beyond enrollment: The causal effect of need-based grants on college access, persistence, and graduation. *Journal of Labor Economics*, 34(4). OnlineFirst July 2016.

Chronicle of Higher Education. (2020). Chronicle of Higher Education 2020–2021 Almanac. Gender, Race & Ethnicity of Noninstructional Staff Members, by Employment Status, Fall 2018: 2-year public institutions.

Clark, B. R. (1968). The "cooling out" function revisited. *New Directions for Community Colleges*, 32(Spring), 15–31.

Cohen, A. (1974). Political influences and curriculum and instruction. *New Directions in Community Colleges*. 7(Autumn), 39–53. doi:10.1002/cc.36819740706.

Cohen, A. M., Brawer, F. B. & Kisker, C. B. (2014). *The American community college*. Sixth Edition. Jossey-Bass.

Dougherty, K., Lahr, H., & Morest V. S. (2017). Reforming the American Community College: Promising changes and their challenges. CCRC Working Paper No.98. Teachers College, Columbia, University, New York.

Fink, J., & Jenkins, D. (2020). Shifting sectors: How a commonly used federal datapoint undercounts over a million community college students. The Mixed Methods blog. April 30, 2020. https://ccrc.tc.columbia.edu/easyblog/shifting-sectors-community-colleges-undercounting.html.

Goldrick-Rab, S., Kelchen, R., Harris, D. N., & Benson, J. (2016). Reducing income inequality in educational attainment: Experimental evidence on the impact of financial aid on college completion. *American Journal of Sociology*, 121(6), 1762–1817. doi:10.1086/685442.

Hu, X. (2020). Building an equalized technology-mediated advising structure: Academic advising at community colleges in the post-COVID-19 era. *Community College Journal of Research and Practice*. Published Online: 28 Jul 2020.

Irwin, J., & Oakley, E. O. (2018). Trust students, not tests, to open pathway to community college success. https://edsource.org/2018/trust-students-not-tests-to-open-pathway-to-community-college-success/596996.

Jencks, C., & Riesman, D. (1968). *The academic revolution*. Double Day.

Jenkins, D., & Fink, J. (2016). *The effectiveness of helping community college students attain bachelor's degrees*. Community College Research Center, Teachers College, Columbia University.

Karabel, J. (1972). Community colleges and social stratification. *Harvard Educational Review*, 42(4), 521–562.

Lichtenberger, E. L., & Dietrich, C. (2017). The community college penalty? Examining the bachelor's completion rates of community college transfer students as a function of time. *Community College Review*, 45(1), 3–32.

Long, A. (2016). *Overcoming educational racism in the community college: Creating pathways to success for minority and impoverished student populations*. Stylus.

O'Banion, T. (2019). *13 Ideas that are transforming the community college world*. Rowman and Littlefield.

Page, L. C., & Scott-Clayton, J. (2015, December). Improving college access in the United States: Barriers and policy responses. NBER Working Paper No. 21781. https://www.preceden.com/timelines/27002-history-of-the community-college.

Pew Research Center. (2019). Community college student completion. https://www.pewresearch.org/.

Pfeffer, F. T., & Goldrick-Rab, S. (2014). The community college effect revisited: The importance of attending to heterogeneity and complex counterfactuals. *Sociological Science* 1, 448–466. http://fabianpfeffer.com/wp-content/uploads/BrandPfefferGoldrick-Rab2014.pdf.

Raby, R. L., & Valeau, E.J. (2009). *Community college models: Globalization and higher education reform.* Edited by R. L. Raby & E. J. Valeau. Springer.

Schneider, M., & Yin, L. M. (2012). *Completion matters: The high cost of low community college graduation rates.* American Enterprise Institute for Public Policy Research. http://199.87.225.222/ournextbigidea/documents/5_Completion_Matters.pdf.

Shapiro, D., Dundar, A., Wakhungu, P.K., Yuan, X., Nathan, A., & Hwang, Y. (2016, November). Completing college: A national view of student attainment rates – Fall 2010 Cohort (Signature Report No. 12). National Student Clearinghouse Research Center. https://nscresearchcenter.org/signaturereport12/.

Tandberg, D. A., Hillman, N., & Barakat, M. (2014). State higher education performance funding for community colleges: Diverse effects and policy Implications. *Teachers College Record*, 116(12). https://eric.ed.gov/?id=EJ1044657.

Van Noy, M., & Zeidenberg, M. (2017). Community college pathways to the STEM workforce: What are they, who follows them, and how? *New Directions for Community Colleges*, 178(Summer), 9–21. doi:10.1002/cc.20249.

Wang, X. (2013). Why students choose STEM majors: Motivation, high school learning, and postsecondary context of support. *American Educational Research Journal*, 50(5), 1081–1121. doi:10.3102/0002831213488622.

Xu, W., & Trimble, M. J. (2015). What about certificates? Evidence on the labor market returns to non-degree community college award in two states. *Educational Evaluation and Policy Analysis*, 38(2), 272–292.

Zook, G. (1947). *The president's commission on higher education: Higher education for American democracy.* U. S. Government Printing Office.

Part II

# Building Leverage to Get the Job

Chapter Six

# Steps to the Presidency

## A Basic Review

This chapter closely looks at five popular and tried ways in which aspirants engage to get to the presidency position.

### DOCTORAL EDUCATION

The road to the presidency is influenced significantly by the possession of a doctorate. In 1984, 76% of community college presidents had earned doctorates (Vaughan, 1986) that rose to 87% in 2002 (Duree, 2007) and to 98% in 2015 (O'Banion, 2011). In the last century, McFarlin et al. (1999) found that exceptional presidents had a background in the study of higher education. Moore et al. (1985) revealed that presidents had earned their degrees through Educational Leadership programs. Today, the specifically designed Community College Leadership programs are equally accessible (Eddy & Kirby, 2020; Romero & Purdy, 2004) and have become essential (Romano et al., 2009). There is equal weight given to those who obtain a Doctor of Philosophy (PhD) or an Education Doctorate (EdD) degree.

Traditional academic doctoral degrees serve as filters in alerting hiring consultants, boards of trustees, and human resources departments of potential leaders (Amey et al., 2002; Eddy & Kirby, 2020; McFarlin et al., 1999; Moore et al., 1985; Vineyard, 1993). I conducted a review of 100+ job openings between 2015 and 2020, as listed in the Chronicle of Higher Education. In the review, 90% gave the preferred preference to an earned doctorate. The degree signifies a higher level of acquired knowledge that supposes the candidate is scholarly, articulate in writing and speech, conversant with the latest trends, and has the discipline to lead others. The dissertation itself is seen as an excellent culmination of the process of building critical analysis skills. Published scholarship, especially in highly ranked academic journals, is increasingly important to demonstrate academic strength and leadership.

The doctoral degree's importance emanates from the foundations of the presidents' pathway beginning with faculty ranks. Since faculty were scholars and in the university scholars possessed PhDs, such scholarship came to be expected of the community college leaders. In this century, there is a notable shift in the awarding and thinking of the terminal degree. It is influenced more by grantors' and employers' need for credentialing, professional training, and advanced training. Preparation for either degree is governed by accrediting agencies and their demand for accountability and measurable outcomes (Winter & Griffiths, 2000). The degree is tailored to meet the consumers' needs, and future leaders must respond to those wishes if they plan to remain employed.

Finally, earning a doctoral degree is personally, academically, and mentally a formidable challenge and will significantly impact one's family, career, and personal life. It is very disruptive, monetarily costly, and has no guarantee of getting a good return on investment. However, candidates who expect to be competitive in today's market need the doctorate, and not because it will make them a better leader but because nearly every serious competitor has one or is on a track to earning one. In simple terms, the terminal degree is a union card and makes the candidate eligible to compete on the open market.

## PROFESSIONAL DEVELOPMENT

The need for continuing education serves as a filter in hiring choices due to quality assurance qualifications embedded in these programs. Early researchers (Anderson, 1997; Anderson, et. al., 2002; McCarthy, 1999; McFarlin & Ebbers, 1998; Moore, 1998, Vaughan & Wiseman 1988; Wallin, 2002) documented that human capital investment, including participating in professional development, heavily and positively influence career advancement. I concur that individuals who expand their experiences and competencies through participation in recognized training programs or activities are more attractive as a presidential candidate than those just having a doctorate. Even though it will satisfy the specified requirements commonly advertised in most presidential job announcements, it alone merely contributes to addressing the job requirements. This section shares several options for professional development.

## Grow your Own Programs

Grow Your Own Programs are generally established by the president and offered to interested or promising prospects on a volunteer or assigned basis. They contain information on a variety of topics that include team building, management, leadership styles, issues specific to the institution, and real-life situations beyond anecdotal evidence that are grounded in the specific college offering the programs (Benard & Piland, 2014; Jeandron, 2006; Reille & Kezar, 2010). The American Association of Community Colleges (AACC) has a framework for lesson plans for these programs, which has been adopted by colleges nationwide.

## AACC Leadership Programs

The AACC added a particular module to leadership training programs to explore the necessary competencies for leadership. The competencies listed in this program are now recognized as the agreed-upon skills required to transform the existing college infrastructure and as those that would allow an individual to adeptly foster reforms that would ensure student success (AACC, 2005, 2013, 2020). AACC works with several councils nationwide to teach these competencies. For example, the *AACC Futures Leaders Institute* (2018) has affiliations with the National Council on Black American Affairs Leadership Development Institute for African American Mid-level Administrators, National Community College Hispanic Council Leadership Fellows Program, National Asian Pacific Islander Council, and American Association for Women in Community Colleges. Other councils also offer programs, including the National Council for Learning Resources, Council for the Study of Community Colleges, National Coalition of Advanced Technology Centers, Community College Business Officers, and National Council for Student Development. The advantage of networking allows each affiliation to provide their own interpretations of the competencies that work best for its constituencies.

## Aspen Institute College Excellence Program

Aspen Institute College Excellence Program (2020) is a nonprofit educational and policy studies organization based in Washington, DC. It fosters leadership training based on enduring values and provides a nonpartisan venue for dealing with critical issues. The Aspen Presidential Fellowship for Community College Excellence (2020) aims to develop a cadre of exceptional leaders who can transform community colleges to achieve higher student success levels while maintaining broad access.

Drawing on excellent community colleges' exemplary work, the Institute engages a select group of Fellows each year in an intensive, applied leadership executive program, delivered in collaboration with the Stanford Educational Leadership Initiative. The year-long fellowship includes three in-person residential seminars plus structured mentoring by experienced community college presidents and developing a strategic leadership vision through a capstone project. The Aspen Presidential Fellowship centers on three broad themes: Leading for Impact, Leading Transformational Change, and Partnering for Collective Action.

## Harvard Institutes for Higher Education

The Harvard Institutes for Higher Education (2020a) the Gran-daddy of them all is an intensive residential program that shares new ideas and insights on efficient management practice in higher education. There are three separate institutes offered at Harvard University that are aimed at mid- and senior-level administrators: (1) Institute for Educational Management (IEM) is designed for senior-level administrators who are responsible for shaping broad institutional policy; (2) Institute for Management and Leadership in Education (MLE) program is designed for skilled, experienced administrators, such as deans and directors, provosts, and vice presidents who will help their institutions adapt to a changing future; and (3) Manage Development Program (MDP) is for the mid-level administrators in their first seven years of responsible leadership position. Besides, there is a stand-alone *Harvard Seminar for Experienced Presidents* (2020b) that offers a rare opportunity for presidents to step back from the daily responsibilities of the presidency and discuss key leadership issues in a confidential setting and reflect on choices that lie ahead of them and their institution. The Seminar focuses on critical issues facing their institution, including crisis leadership, fundraising, the role of new technologies and online education, initiating change and overcoming barriers, and personal planning about their presidency.

## American Council on Education Institute for New Chief Academic Officers

The American Council on Education (ACE) (2020a) Institute for New Chief Academic Officers provides practical executive leadership development for those in their first three years on the job. Participants are joined by experienced Chief Academic Officers and presidents who facilitate conversations and serve as resources. The intent is to provide participants with an understanding of how common issues and challenges play out in different types of institutions, different and competing perspectives from peers with different experiences, lessons, and insights about leadership challenges faced by Chief Academic Officers across-sections of the institution.

*The ACE Institute for New Presidents* (2020b) consists of two in-person meetings that are highly participatory, with sessions facilitated by experienced and successful presidents that identify topics and issues of immediate concern to new presidents and provide the means to address them. Topics focus on challenges faced by new presidents; knowledge and skills for dealing with high-visibility, high-exposure, and unexpected challenges and opportunities; practical advice on working effectively with the media; increased understanding of how to assess and manage campus culture and change processes; practical advice on how to form and manage a highly effective executive team; an extended professional network of fellow presidents from a cross-section of institutions; and a low-risk setting to test ideas.

### Association of California Community College Administrators Mentor Program

The Association of California Community College Administrators (2020) created a year-long Mentor Program in 1983 (Valeau, 1999; Valeau & Boggs, 2004) to focus on skill-building and collaborative learning. For over 30 years, the program has focused on enhancing mid-level managers' career opportunities to prepare them to think about and then engage in the president position pathway. The program is supported by a volunteer corps of mid- and senior-level administrators that function as mentors in service to aspirants interested in ascending to the presidency. Participants are selected based on a proven demonstration of the potential for expanded leadership roles and responsibilities in their current or future responsibilities with the California community college system. Those in the program become part of the networking in inter-regional focus throughout the state and across the nation.

## TEACHING EXPERIENCE

Most search committees want candidates to have some teaching experience, preferably at the community college level. According to Vaughan (1989), the traditional leadership pathways begin with being a faculty member and then proceeds through a succession of community college administrative posts below the presidential level. This pathway remains the most popular today. There are community college administrators who do not have faculty experience and work their way to a presidency through a succession of community college administrative posts below the presidential level. These candidates often use part-time teaching experience to respond to job announcements that ask for "teaching experience."

## DEMONSTRATED YEARS OF SERVICE

Search committees value candidates who have demonstrated years of service, preferably at the community college level, and relevant administrative experience at least to a Dean or Vice President level (Barwick, 2002; Kubala & Bailey, 2001). Moore et al. (1985) defined administrative experiences as including academic-related matters, student services, administrative services, and financing. Vineyard (1993b) added the importance of specific experience as an academic administrator, a student personnel administrator, or a counselor. Binder (2000) describes the Dean's position as "slapping on training wheels," and Weltsch (2009) notes that the chances of becoming a president are upwards tenfold following the role of Dean. Today, 84–90% of community college presidents began as a Chief Academic Officer (ACE, 2017). However, as noted, a new and smaller generation of presidents gained their position without serving in other nontraditional pathways. In response to our time's changing sociocultural and economic challenges, experiences in public relations training, social media training, accounting, and business management are incredibly beneficial as emerging skills. Thus, those who come from the institution's business sector will have essential and unique skill sets.

## MENTORSHIP

There is no widely accepted definition of a mentor. Sometimes it is viewed as a person who can arrange opportunities and experiences with others for a protégée in relationship to their aspirations. Sometimes it can help one navigate the terrain of the job, including its pitfalls. It is someone who can make a phone call, clear a path, give direction, and provide counsel and advice that aids in decision-making related to important career decisions. At other times, it can be an experienced person in their field who can introduce you to people you need to know and who need to know you. Finally, it can be someone who teaches you to manage certain situations and be a guiding force in your development. Regardless of definition, the process of mentoring is highly valued (Eddy et al., 2007; Merriam & Thomas, 1986).

Central in the discussion of gaining the community college presidency is the need to be mentored by a sitting community college president. Sitting presidents often single out individuals from outside associations or within their institutions as good prospects. In the early 2000s, it was estimated that about 33% of community college presidents were internal candidates (Cooper & Pagotto, 2003). It is argued that there is strength from pulling from within. This process bodes well for internal candidates and ensures smooth transitioning from an existing faculty and/or staff position. Another benefit is the maintaining of the status quo. This strategy, however, has some downsides. It can often cause resentment among colleagues in the ranks who do not see themselves being offered the same attention for whatever reason. It also closes the door to talented applicants when word seeps out that the inside candidate is the odds-on favorite to get the advertised job. Finally, sometimes it is useful to go outside the institution to use the mentorship to bring in new talent that might initiate a new and inspired vision and direction for the college.

While little data exist on the impact a mentoring style has on the success of the protégé, the literature consistently mentions the importance of a mentor. It is echoed by the Buttimer awardees and the Sitting Presidents who were interviewed for this book and who collectively confirmed the importance of having a champion who can guide one and in whom one can confide. Another benefit often shared from Sitting Presidents who are women or leaders of color is that mentoring was an essential component of their career advancement. It provided the opportunity for intergenerational transfer of essential skills, knowledge, and behaviors (Edgecomb, 2019). Thus, mentoring helps to contribute to qualified applicants' gender and racial diversification for senior-level administrative positions. The lesson is the need to have someone willing to help one realize and identify their strengths and weaknesses, help them manage either one or act as advocates committed to helping one achieve their goals. Moreover, the person would have the courage and confidence to give an unequivocal yes to any college interested in hiring is invaluable.

## Types of Mentoring

Mentoring occurs on two levels – Unplanned or Formal. Unplanned mentoring is when the recipient finds someone who is naturally interested in their career and wants to champion their growth. Precisely, they appear willing to help the protégé in forging links and contacts and assist them in understanding leadership roles, management, and teaching technical skills for short- and long-term success. Above all, the person needs to be a dedicated advocate and supporter (Valeau & Boggs, 2004).

Formal mentoring occurs through engagement in a specific association or statewide leadership development program in which a mentor is assigned. Some of the association programs focus on different aspects of mentoring. The ACE Fellow model focuses on skills training and competencies development. The Aspen Presidential Fellowship focuses on vision and leadership competencies intended to transform the college. The Association of California Community Colleges Administrators mentoring program focuses on mentoring as a tool to socialize, expand known competencies, and mitigate residual effects on combating racism and sexism.

Despite the importance of mentoring, not all relationships are positive. A mentoring relationship can be weakened when issues and concerns never get addressed between the parties because of either party's eagerness to act/serve in a specific and prescribed manner for whatever reason. As a result, opportunities in the process are often lost. The following are points of reference for effective mentoring. First, choose wisely whom you plan to follow and whom you allow to lead you. Ultimately, you are the captain of your ship, and whether it sails smoothly or not is a function of one's decision-making and being mentored is a significant step. Second, engage in self-introspection by asking: (a) What are my needs, strengths, and tolerance for receiving and following the advice offered? (b) Are you committed to taking direction and advice that is contrary to your perceived needs or interest? (c) Critically assess whom you choose to be the mentor by asking:

- Is the mentor respected in the field? Is the mentor trustworthy?
- Is the mentor seriously committed to helping you achieve your goals?
- Is the mentor giving assignments or projects that are timely and relevant?
- Is race a preference of the mentor?
- Does the mentor have the time for collaboration?
- Is the mentor comfortable with who you are and your agenda?
- Is the mentor committed to increasing your exposure in his/her inner and outer circles?

## SUMMARY

Scholarship is consistent in agreeing that the most common pathways to the presidency have remained mostly unchanged for the past 25 years (Amey et al., 2002; Boggs, 1989; Cook, 2012; Wiseman, & Vaughan 2002). Literature also focuses on targeting and then educating the next generation from mid-level administrative positions (Ebbers et al., 2010; Raby & Valeau, 2019). Based on my observations as a CEO Search Consultant for over a decade, today, as in yesterday, candidates need to plan for ascendency by focusing on personal and professional growth. Future candidates need to get their doctorate, establish a peer network, be willing to move to a new town, and accept a less than ideal locale. On the professional level, future candidates need to get into the academic or student services pipeline, starting with part- or full-time teaching, counseling, and then focus on moving into division chair and then to other academic leaderships or student services leadership roles. Also, candidates need to assume leadership roles on campus actively and be prepared to accept mentoring.

## REFERENCES

American Association of Community Colleges (AACC). (2005). *Competency framework for community college leaders.* http://www.aacc.nche.edu/competency_framework/pdf.

American Association of Community Colleges (AACC). (2013). *Competencies for community college leaders.* Second Edition. AACC. www.aacc.nche.edu/newsevents/Events/leadershipsuite/Documents/AACC/CoreCompetencies/web.pdf.

American Association of Community Colleges (AACC). (2018). AACC leadership suite. https://www.aacc.nche.edu/events/aacc-leadership-suite/.

American Association of Community Colleges (AACC). (2020). *Competencies for community college leaders.* Third Edition. www.aacc.nche.edu/publications-news/aacc competencies-for-community-college-leaders/.

American Council on Education. (2017). Comprehensive demographic profile of American college presidents shows slow progress in diversifying leadership ranks. www.acenet.edu/news-room/Pages/Comprehensive-Demographic Profile-of-American-College-Presidents-Shows-Slow-Progress-in-Diversifying-Leadership- Ranks.aspx.

American Council on Education. (2020a). Institute for new chief academic officers. https://ace-institute-for-new-chief-academic-officers/.

American Council on Education. (2020b). Institute for new presidents. https://ace-institute-for-new-presidents/.

Amey, M., VanDerLinden, K., & Brown, D. (2002). Perspectives on community college leadership: Twenty years in the making. *Community College Journal of Research and Practice*, 26(7–8), 573–589. doi:10.1080/10668920276018l805.

Anderson, P., Murray, J. P., & Olivarez, A. (2002). The managerial roles of public community college Chief Academic Officers. *Community College Review*, 30(2), 1–26. doi:10.1177/009155210203000201.

Aspen Institute. (2020). Aspen presidential fellowship community college excellence program. www.aspeninstitute/org/presidential-fellowship-community-college-excellence/.

Association of California Community College Administrators. (2020). Mentor program. www.acca.org/mentor_program/.

Barwick, J. T. (2002). Pathways to the presidency: Same trail, new vistas. *Community College Journal*, 73(1), 6–11.

Benard, M. K., & Piland, W. E. (2014). Case study of a community college grow your own (GYO) leaders program. *Journal of Applied Research in the Community College*, 21(2), 21–28.

Binder, F. M. (2000). So you want to be a college president?" *COSMOS Journal*. www./smosclub.org/journals/2000/binder.html.

Boggs, G. R. (1989). Pathways to the presidency. *AACJC Journal*, June/July, 41–45.

Cook, B. J. (2012). The American college president study: Key findings and takeaways. *American Council on Education*. www.acenet.edu/the-presidency/columns-and-features/Pages/The-American-College-President- Study.aspx.

Cooper, J. E., & Pagotto, L. (2003). Developing community college faculty as leaders. *New Directions for Community Colleges*, 123, 27–37.

Duree, C. (2007). The challenge of the community college presidency in the new millennium: Pathways, preparation, competencies, and leadership programs needed to survive. [Unpublished doctoral dissertation]. Iowa State University.

Ebbers, L., Conover, K. S., & Samuels, A. (2010). Leading from the middle: Preparing leaders for new roles. *New Directions in Community Colleges*, 149(Spring), 59–64.

Eddy, P. L., & Kirby, E. (2020). *Leading for tomorrow: A primer for succeeding in higher education leadership*. Rutgers University Press.

Eddy, L. T., Rhodes, J. E., & Allen, T. D. (2007). Definition and evolution of mentoring. In *The Blackwell handbook of mentoring: A multiple perspectives approach*. Edited by T. Allen & L. Edy (pp. 7–20). Blackwell Publishing.

Edgecomb, N. (2019). Demography as opportunity. In *13 ideas that are transforming the community college world*. Edited by T. U. O'Banion (pp. 213–231). Roman & Littlefield.

Harvard Institutes. (2020a). Harvard institutes for higher education: Institute for educational management (IEM). Homepage. https://www.gse.harvard.edu/ppe/program/institute-educational-management-iem.

Harvard Institutes. (2020b). Harvard Seminar for Experienced Presidents. Homepage. https://www.gse.harvard.edu/ppe/program/harvard-seminar-presidential-leadership.

Jeandron, C. A. (2006). *Growing your own leaders: Community colleges step up*. Community College Press.

Kubala, T. S., & Bailey, G. M. (2001). A new perspective on community college presidents: Results of a national study. *Community College Journal of Research and Practice*, 25(6), 793–804.

McCarthy, M. (1999). The evolution of educational leadership preparation programs. In *Handbook of Research on Educational Administration*. Second Edition. Edited by J. Murphy, & K. S. Louis (pp. 119–139). Jossey-Bass.

McFarlin, C. H., Crittenden, B. J., & Ebbers, L. H. (1999). Background factors common among outstanding community college presidents. *Community College Review*, 27(3), 19–31.

McFarlin, C. H., & Ebbers, L. (1998). Preparation factors common in outstanding community college presidents. *Michigan Community College Journal*, 4(1), 33–47.

Merriam, S. B., & Thomas, T. K. (1986). The role of mentoring in the career development of community college presidents. *Community/Junior College Quarterly*, 10, 177–191.

Moore, K. (1998). Administrative careers. In *Leaders for a New Era*. Edited by M. Green (pp. 159–180). Macmillan.

Moore, K., Martorana, S., & Twombly, S. (1985). *Today's academic leaders: A national study of administrators in two-year colleges*. Center for the Study of Higher Education.

O'Banion, T., Weidner, L., & Wilson, C. (2011). Creating a culture of innovation in the community college. *Community College Journal of Research and Practice*, 35(6), 470–483. doi:10.1080/10668926.2010.515508.

Raby, R. L., & Valeau, E.J. (2019). Position training and succession planning for community college international education leaders. *Community College Journal of Research and Practice*. On-LineFirst. Published July 26, 2019. doi:10.1080/10668926.2019.1645055.

Reille, A., & Kezar, A. (2010, July). Balancing the pros and cons of community college "Grow-your-own" leadership programs. *Community College Review*, 38(1), 59–81.

Romano, R. M., Townsend, B., & Mamiseishvili, K. (2009). Leaders in the making: Profile and perceptions of students in community college doctoral programs. *Community College Journal of Research and Practice*, 33(3), 309–320.

Romero, M., & Purdy, L. (2004, February/March). The community college leadership development institute. *Community College Journal*, 74(2), 32–34.

Valeau, E. J. (1999). Mentoring: The association of California community colleges project. *Community College Review*, 27(3), 33–46.

Valeau, E. J., & Boggs, G. R. (2004). An assessment of the association of California community college administrators mentor program. *Community College Review*, 31(4), 48–46. doi:10.1177/009155210403100403.

Vaughan, G. B. (1986). *The Community college presidency*. American Council on Education/Macmillan.

Vaughan, G. B. (1989). *Leadership in transition: The community college presidency*. American Association of Community Colleges.

Vaughan, G., & Wiseman, I. (1998). *The community college presidency at the millennium*. The Community College Press.

Vineyard, E. E. (1993). The administrator's role in staff management. In *Managing Community Colleges: A Handbook for Effective Practice*. Edited by M. Cohen, & F. Brawer (pp. 363–381). Jossey-Bass.

Wallin, D. L. (2002). Professional development for presidents: A study of community and technical college presidents in three states. *Community College Review*, 30(2), 27–41.

Weltsch, M. D. (2009). A study of community college presidential qualifications and career paths. [Unpublished Doctoral Dissertation] Kansas State University.

Winter, R., & Griffiths, K. (2000). The "academic" qualities of practice: What are the criteria for a practice-based Ph.D.? *Studies in Higher Education*, 25, 25–37.

Wiseman, I. M., & Vaughan, G. B. (2002). *The community college presidency, 2001*. (Report No. AACC-RB-02-1; AACC Ser-3). American Association of Community Colleges.

# Chapter Seven

# Understanding the Context

The presidency's journey begins with self-introspection regarding wanting the position. It extends to fully understanding the college or district's political context and then finally understanding the community's and businesses' educational needs.

## HAVE THE DESIRE

It is generally folklore with a great deal of truth among veteran community college presidents that the presidency is a contact sport wherein players must desire and enjoy participating. Despite national conferences that market the position's accessibility, the role is not for everyone due to the difficulty of the job and its toll on one's mental and physical well-being. Like the Buttimer awardee recipients and Sitting Presidents interviewed for this book, I agree that desire begins the journey in which one recognizes in oneself a wish or firm intention for change. The journey continues with self-reflection regarding skills and abilities to manage high-level responsibilities and lead an organization. It also includes one's durability, given the average tenure of a college president, which hovers between five and seven years. The reality of understanding the presidency result in discovering that one may not possess the requisite skill or temperament. Such reflection requires a focus on an honest assessment of your chances of success, which today are similar to what they were a decade ago. Even the percentages of success are similar to what Charles Thwing (1926) shared: when reviewing the presidency, 15% are successful to a high degree and 10% are failures.

## UNDERSTAND THE FIELD

Aspirants should know the many challenges that intersect with leading a community college. Boggs and McPhail (2016) and O'Banion (2019) describe potential issues presidents will face in the future and continuously question their abilities, leadership goals and talents. These include: (a) transparency and accountability that align with state and federal agencies accreditation policies that link dollars to measurable student outcomes; (b) expanding Board Creep where boards overreach when it comes to their authority, responsibility, and leadership; (c) expanding influence by faculty unions who are successfully winning Board seats to control the agenda and decision-making processes while knowingly embedding the ability to micromanage the president; (d) devaluation of the degree as the card to good-paying jobs when placed into the context of increasing student debt; (e) movement toward certification of skills demonstrating what a person can do; (f) meeting the educational, social, and emotional needs of expanded student diversity that does not always match the diversity of those in leadership positions; (g) sexual assault and discrimination on campuses; (h) cybersecurity threats; and (i) systemic racism and fractured politics along racial, ethnic, and vociferous political lines. Managing such challenges in an environment where social media is dominant requires diligence and focus.

## COMPETING DEMANDS

There are competing demands between and within the various stakeholders of the organization. Most important, however, the office and the president are coexisting personalities with a long historical base. You are merely one player in a lengthy line of many other players who have come and gone from the institution that selects you as their next leader.

### Multiple Missions Demands

Community colleges are known for their multiple missions. They exist to serve the college's various needs and respond to the increasingly complicated environments they are situated in (Bailey & Morest, 2004; Dougherty & Townsend, 2006). Current discussions point to the inefficiency of multiple missions, the inadequacy of resources to meet the multiple missions, and the conflict that arises when one mission is positioned over another, and negatively affect students (Barranger & Jaquette, 2018). Some institutions are choosing not to be a comprehensive institution (Hornak & Garza Mitchell, 2016). Irrespective, the president needs to champion which missions to focus on regarding college curriculum and programming.

## President Demands

The president is the leader and subject to earned and unearned interpretations that often result in criticisms by all constituent groups across the organization. These criticisms often can imperil the president and end her presidency at that particular institution. As Prather (1963) explains, the president is Saint or Satan, depending on the president's favor or denies. The president's activities and decisions are central to the interpretation of the campus's philosophy in which the college's mission is influenced by institutional history and culture. The job is laborious, time-consuming, repetitive at times, and demands attention and transparency. The president is the institution's defender and is expected by all subordinates to come to their rescue in time of need, even when they are undeserving. Even in a valiant attempt to do so, the critics will still find something to criticize.

## Funding and Governance Demands

Traditionally, community college funding has been primarily based on local income tax and federal support. In this century, however, the amount of national and state funding has decreased substantially. As a result, many colleges are and remain underfunded and overwhelmed by doing more with less. Moreover, during periods of economic crisis, the local income tax is also challenged, limiting funding flows. Policymakers have proven unwilling or unable to find sustainable strategies that can enable appropriate funding. Chronic underfunding challenges the college's ability to educate today's citizenry (Pfeffer & Goldrick-Rabb, 2014). Entrepreneurial programs have become a necessity to try to find new funding to help keep the colleges afloat.

## Board Demands

Boards of trustees have fiduciary responsibility for the districts that they serve. The trustees are accountable for establishing and monitoring policies and procedures that help to govern the college and oversee responsibly in concert with the president. Beyond necessary planning and oversight duties, boards of trustees address such challenges as tuition, affordability, job placement for graduates, quality of education, competition with other institutions and online learning programs, fundraising, legislative mandates, media, and budgeting and planning. They represent the paying public who entrusts them to oversee the proper and successful function of their asset, i.e., the college and the district. The Board often faces tremendous pressure from the community for the image and success of the college while operating in a social and political culture, where demands are expected and where presidents are accountable to a wide array of constituencies all wanting something from the asset. As such, Boards are apt to get involved in matters best managed by the president, who must always work to help the board be as effective and efficient as possible. When relationships break down, it can negatively impact the institution, thereby affecting its effectiveness and image throughout the community and, on some levels, the state. When Boards show disruptive behavior that pits themselves against the president, they are famously dubbed "Rogue Trustees" (O'Banion, 2009). A significant challenge for the president is to become even more skilled at collaborating with the Board to promote harmony and, ultimately, institutional success. Such a task is wearisome because it demands a significant amount of attention, skill, and even luck. Aspirants need to know that the board and the presidents are partners, but the board has the ultimate authority. In turn, the Board needs to confidently entrust its authority to the president's leadership and skillful management. Thus, they expect to collaborate with leaders who embody competency, integrity, trust, loyalty, and civility.

## Faculty Demands

Faculty are a key constituent group. Through a system called participatory governance and unionism linked to employee bargaining, faculty are vital contributors to the decision-making process in academic and professional matters. It includes their voice in developing and implementing curriculum, grading policies, student learning objectives, degree requirements, accreditation standards, faculty qualifications, professional development, and faculty training. In many community colleges, faculty pay close attention to these areas and fiercely guard their ownership. In some contexts, faculty may demand more involvement and power in the college's operation and administration than the president prefers. While some of these situations work well to promote significant change, there is an underlying belief that few faculty are up to being accountable for assuming the responsibility that goes along with having more accountability and power. As a result, presidents must walk a fine line in these matters, especially when they do not endorse a group's recommendation even if it is favorable to the institution (Birnbaum, 2004). Sometimes when tensions spiral out of control, the president can quickly receive a vote of no confidence from the faculty, leading to their dismissal by the board and, worse yet, a ruined career.

## Classified Staff Demands

The classified staff also participates in the participatory-governance process. Classified staff expects the president to address issues of concern to them, particularly in areas of salaries, working conditions, participation in decision-making, and, most importantly, fairness and equity. The latter is essential because classified staff on most college campuses feel disrespected and view themselves as having a lower status than the faculty. The president must remain the focal point and equally examine all matters presented as potential conflicts and opportunities. In turn, the president must demonstrate consistent leadership that is transparent, fair, equitable, and beneficial to the college and all stakeholders.

## Student Demands

Chessman and Wayt (2016) suggest that colleges and universities across the United States and Canada have in this decade experienced the most significant upsurge in student activism since the 1960s. Students are demanding changes in the review and revision of institutional policies and practices affecting campus climate and diversity practices and are presenting transparent leadership plans of action. Also, they are demanding more resources to be allocated to the needs of diverse and marginalized students, including academic, career, legal, and mental health support, increases in diversity across the campus community, new or revised diversity or cultural competency training, and calls for revisions or additions to the curricula to include diverse perspectives. Other issues that impact student demands are the availability of financial aid for specific college costs, college-free tuition, the percentage of students graduating, athletics and sports teams, and international educational programming. As drivers of change, students in each generation will continue to use their voices to advocate for meaningful change. The 2019–2020 academic year activism shows the intensity in which students are demanding changes educationally and in the society.

## Community and Business Community Demands

The local and business communities also have an interest in the success of the college. Families in the community want education accessible and relevant to their children's needs and expect a return on their investment. The New America's Education Policy Program (2019) survey of 1,011 prospective community college students aged 16–40 confirmed that the top reasons to go to college were: (1) to improve employment opportunities;

(2) to make more money; and (3) to get a good job. The community's demands are directly related to the academic and technical programs offered by the college. The business community needs a trained workforce and views the community college as a significant source for their needs. They invest in college programming, development, and training. Through the partnership with the colleges, they identify emerging fields, technologies, and jobs. Concurrently, they want the college to graduate a trained, certified workforce to meet their workforce needs and demands. The business community holds the college accountable and generally work with the leadership to ensure institutional success and effectiveness. They are powerful, influential forces that are business-minded and expect a return on their investment. Finally, they are collaborators in fundraising and other entrepreneurial projects vital to the colleges' image, relevance, and success.

## REFERENCES

Bailey, T., & Morest, V. S. (2004). *The organizational efficiency of multiple missions for community colleges.* Community College Research Center. https://ccrc.tc.columbia.edu/publications/organizational-efficiency-multiple-missions.html.

Barranger, S. N., & Jaquette, O. (2018). The moving missions of community colleges: An examination of degree-granting profiles over time. *Community College Review*, 46(12). Online First. doi:10.1177/0091552118786012.

Birnbaum, R. (2004). The end of shared governance: Looking ahead or looking back. *New Directions for Higher Education*, 127, 5–22.

Boggs, G. R., & McPhail, C. J. (2016). *Practical leadership in community colleges: Navigating today's challenges.* John Wiley and Sons/Jossey-Bass.

Chessman, H., & Wayt, L. (2016). What are students demanding. HigherEd Today. www.higheredtoday.org/2016/01/13/what-are-student- demanding/.

Dougherty, K. J., & Townsend, B. K. (2006). Community college missions: A theoretical and historical perspective. *New Directions for Community Colleges*, 136, 5–13.

Hornak, A. M., & Garza Mitchell, R. L. (2016). Changing times, complex decisions. *Community College Review*, 44(2), 119–194. doi:10.1177/0091552116629548.

New America's Educational Policy Program Education. (2019). College decisions. https://www.new america.org/education-policy/edcentral/collegedecisions/.

O'Banion, T. (2009). *The rouge trustee: The elephant in the room. League for innovation in the community college.* The University of Michigan.

O'Banion, T. (2019). *13 Ideas that are transforming the community college world*. Rowman and Littlefield.

Pfeffer, F. T., & Goldrick-Rab, S. (2014). The community college effect revisited: The importance of attending to heterogeneity and complex counterfactuals. *Sociological Science*, 1, 448–466. http://fabianpfeffer.com/wp-content/uploads/BrandPfefferGoldrick-Rab2014.pdf.

Prather, R. (1963). *The college president*. Center for Applied Research in Education, Inc.

Thwing, C. F. (1926). *The college president*. MacMillan.

Chapter Eight

# Develop and Cultivate a Network

One of the most dreaded developmental challenges aspiring leaders in community colleges and higher education generally face is creating a network. Professional and personal contacts are generally made up to provide support, feedback, insight, resources, and information for their assessment and decision-making about many events and circumstances. Included in this chapter are insights for developing and cultivating successful networks.

## OBSTACLES

There are many obstacles to establishing active networks. First, those who rise through the ranks based on their internal comfort zones might believe that success leads to other opportunities. However, success does not occur in isolation. Widely developing and having partnerships and relationships with others inside and outside the organization is tantamount to long-term and ongoing success. Second, some cannot create relational lines that depend less on skills and more on building blocks needed to grow support for decision-making, upward mobility, and in some cases, security. Third, some are unwilling to yield time for cultivation, often because time is in short supply. What complicates this obstacle is that when one cannot see immediate results from their efforts, they will choose not to engage. Fourth, some have ineffective strategies when they are left alone to build their networks and thus lack understanding of networking's intricacies as a step toward the presidency. Fifth, some resist the power of developing networking skills because they believe it is political and leaves them in a vulnerable spot that makes them appear to be needy or weak.

Finally, some resist networking due to their shy personality or have tried networking and did not have a positive experience.

I recall a subordinate as having tremendous skills and talents. This person was very competent but tended to be reserved and withdrawn when out in the crowd. Shaking hands and exchanging pleasantries was awkward, and as a result, social meetings were one that this person tended to avoid when possible. At the same time, they believed that by dropping others' names in power, it would cause them to receive attention and be recognized for their assumed independently strong persona. Their upward progress would be based strictly on talents and skills was the ruling thought. Unfortunately, this subordinate languished in a position for a long time and was stifled. Ultimately, I was asked to provide aid. I introduced the subordinate to leaders who shared similar characteristics in the past and provided a context where knowledge could ground change. In time, this person emerged from a self-imposed shell and started talking less about the names of people they knew and more about what they were doing and their impact and how they were providing pathways for others. Invariably they interviewed for a few positions and eventually ended up as the vice president of a college, where the president and board had assessed them fit for the job they needed to have done.

## NETWORKING TAKES TIME IN ESTABLISHING WHOM YOU KNOW AND WHO KNOWS YOU

Strategically building up one's network takes time. It is conscious behavior focused on cultivation, not manipulation, and prioritizes helping and being helped. It is equally vital to be communal and communicative to embrace moments of being and doing with others. Rhetoric claims that if one wants to ascent higher in their career, it is essential to know someone to get into the door. Instead, I offer that it is not whom you know, but who knows you that matters the most. People across most organizations tend to want to work with someone like themselves and whom they know. This cuts across gender, race, ethnicity, and often geographical boundaries.

Here is a personal case in point. In 1985, I became an American Council on Education fellow (ACE) under the mentorship of A. Robert De Hart, founder and President of De Anza College (California) and one of the country's most respected presidents. Under his tutelage, I gained a suite of leadership skills that guided me to the end of my career. Despite working for three years in various associations inside and outside California, I was unsuccessful in becoming a member of the Association of California Community College Administrators Management Development Commission, a powerful commission across the state. Despite knowing all the players, I was summarily rejected each time I applied. During a mentorship meeting, Bob asked me if I knew what I wanted to do next. I said that I wanted to serve on the Management Development Commission. He immediately called the head of the commission and said these words, "Tom, put Ed on the management development commission." It was done at that moment, and it was not because I knew all the commission members by first names, but because the mentor with power and influence knew me, respected my abilities, and was influential among the decision-makers.

## BUILDING NETWORKS

Networking is challenging. It dictates going beyond one's comfort zone. One must be malleable and prepared to embrace a new philosophy that is genuine and authentic. It is beyond the traditional view of exchanging cards and requires purposeful reaching out, finding common goals, promoting others, and being responsible when called on. Fundamentally, it means creating relationships and using one's ability to communicate with others in various forms and have them understand you. It includes knowing your goals and understanding how to get there, and then cooperating with people who can help because of their knowledge of who you are. The network connects people to people, and it thrives on honesty, respect, integrity, and trust.

Networking occurs every day through casual conversations with people (Alhanati, 2018). In this context, one can network simply with the person sitting closest to you on a plane or to the person standing in line where the conversation is quite casual. Networking can also come from connecting with those from one's past. Thus, outreach to people who previously helped or vice or versa can open new possibilities. One never knows where their good fortune will appear. Above all, it is crucial to stay motivated, focused, and ever open to the possibility of an unexpected opportunity. Purposeful networking involves a conscious practice to connect and to help others periodically and routinely. It should occur equally in the good times as well as in troubled times. Concurrently, it also means collaborating with people in your network who are no longer in power vis-à-vis a position within an organization. These people are respected colleagues and have vast knowledge and contacts, so one should avoid confusing positional status with influence and power. Finally, there is tremendous power in networking through the use of platforms such as LinkedIn, Twitter, Yahoo, and other social media outlets to expand and to cultivate one's network. As it unfolds, one should know their content, work, and above all, have a sense of clarity about what you stand for and what you have to offer to others.

There are two additional and essential networking opportunities not to overlook. First is to build networks (Carnegie, 1981) by taking on leadership roles beyond the campus through national and state organizations. Second, and often overlooked, is collaborating with others to publish. Publications show achievement and intellectual reasoning. Collaborations as a co-author or by working with editors on books, links one to others who are critically engaging in thoughtful and mindful ideas that are highly valued in higher education. They also reveal an ability to present a vision in a scholarly manner, which, in turn, can be read and even quoted by others. It raises visibility as a scholar and as a person of authority. Invariably people will seek to gain further insight into issues of concern, thus widening one's network and creating another level of contacts. As shared before, publishing looks impressive on a résumé when being considered for the college president.

Networking is an ongoing behavior and should not end after the job is secured. Be an active member of the community and demonstrate actions that promote its mission, vision, and values. Inside this cauldron, one is exposed to other people who share common professional interests that, in turn, may be of interest to one's career interests. They can shed some light on one's overall development, thinking, and behavior.

Finally, make ready by knowing and doing your job beyond what is written in the job description. Remember that one's skills and competencies evaluate them as they become the conversation of people talking about you. Know all you can about your job and be interested in the jobs of the people around you. It helps expose you to work inside and outside the organization. It lets people know that one has interest, breadth, and depth. Too frequently, this is overlooked by aspirants who think knowing their job very well is all that matters. It is not! Importantly, cultivating a network is just not building friendships but lending a hand. Remember, networks are a web of colleagues, associates, and friends often dedicated to each other's success. An eager willingness to help someone else should be part of the DNA.

Advisedly, networking is related to building mutual relations with people you respect, trust, and admire. It is not reaching out to everyone, not following others on social media; it is not a social list of friends whom all like each other, and it is not a gossip or rumor mill for the mere sake of sharing stories. Jeannette Purcell (2018) adds that it is also not about attending special events, conferences, or receptions in the hope of making the right connections. Additionally, it is not about arrogance, self-promotion, nor pretending to be something or someone you are not. Importantly, networking is not all about you. Do not exclusively call mentors when you are in trouble or need immediate counsel or help. Such behavior is in poor taste and is sure to cost loss of valued resources. It borders on callously using a person's goodwill and should be avoided at all times. Simply said, stay connected and reach into the network when there are no needs (Ferrazzi & Tahl, 2005).

Visibility is beyond just showing up. Successful networking requires one to be genuine, honest, dependable, and principled. Thus, the network is likely to attract the same kinds of people. Ultimately, one will always be asking people to risk their capital on you as one should be prepared to risk yours on them. Among other things, it is about being comfortably present and understanding that wherever one is, everyone matters. Externally, the myriad of professional organizations in which one participates will be relevant to the network's construction. In all matters, be mindful, be thoughtful, be supportive, and be honest. Act intentionally, and the network will serve everyone quite well. In today's challenging environment undergirded by evolving technology, networking, and sustaining, it is critical for those aspiring to a community college presidency.

## REFERENCES

Alhanati, J. (2018). Who you know might matter more? www.investopedia.com/articles/pf/12.who-we-know.asp.

Carnegie, D. (1981). *How to win friends and influence people.* Simon and Schuster.

Ferrazzi, K., & Tahl, R. (2005). *Never eat alone.* Crown.

Purcell, J. (2018). No-nonsense networking: Six steps to raising your profile. http://jeanettepurcell.com/no-nonsense-networking-six-steps-raising-profile/.

Chapter Nine

# Understanding and Preparing for the Interview Process

The job announcement structure is rooted in a long tradition of colleges and boards engaging their communities, sitting and past presidents, and outside professionals in the field. Hiring agencies take their cues from these announcements and provide additional support in the construction of the announcement. The developed announcement is influenced by historical constructs and guidelines from professionals in the field and associations regarding the CEO's role, function, expectation, leadership, and training needs. This chapter concludes with a critical analysis of why these processes are essential to the applicant.

## COMMUNITY COLLEGE JOB ANNOUNCEMENT: A PROTOTYPE

This sample job description was created based on a review of job descriptions posted from 2015 to 2018 in the *Chronicle of Higher Education*. A job analysis can be used to understand the skills necessary to perform a particular job (Burrus et al., 2013; Rios et al., 2020). Another importance of analyzing online job advertisements is that it requires the hiring committee, in their own words, to precisely list the skills they need from those interested in the presidency position. It is important to note that details will vary depending on district and state policies and regulations. The example below is a fictional account based on facts.

## FLETCHER COMMUNITY COLLEGE JOB ANNOUNCEMENT

The city of Riley has a population of over 900,000 residents. They live in both rural and cosmopolitan areas. Riley County is one of the fastest-growing counties in the state, boasting a diverse population. Less than an hour from the Double Blade Mountains, Riley is the only city in the nation that offers easy access to three national parks: Blues Canyon, Red Rock, and Jade. Seven nearby lakes offer recreational sports nearly year-round, while the mountains allow winter sports such as skiing and snowboarding through day trips or weekend getaways. The city supports 30 theater groups, an opera association, a philharmonic orchestra, 15 museums, and numerous art galleries. Sports enthusiasts can benefit from year-round golf and country clubs of championship caliber. Tennis courts and recreational parks are strategically placed throughout the city. Farmers markets abound with the fresh, just-picked produce grown in the area by local farmers. Baseball fans can see Riley's Double-A baseball club and the Riley Bobcats. Riley will welcome you with open arms with a mild climate conducive to outdoor relaxation, cultural and social enjoyment. The Brave Heart Unified School District has five comprehensive high schools, and a charter high school called the Center for Research and Technology shared with the college district. Brave Heart Unified School District has the highest student test scores in the area, and Fletcher Community College (FCC) has several dual enrollment partnerships with the local school districts.

### The Position

The Chancellor and Board of Trustees of Red Moon Community College District seek a college president for FCC. The new college president will provide unifying and participatory leadership to a dynamic, complex, diverse urban/rural college. The president will build upon the college's strong legacy of achievement and leadership in the community. The college president reports directly to the Chancellor of Red Moon Community College District. The Chancellor and Board of Trustees seek a leader who can facilitate and nurture this climate, even as the college grows and changes.

### The District

Red Moon Community College District was formed in 1945. The district serves approximately one million people and 20 unified and high school districts in more than 5,500 square miles of urban and semi-rural territory that includes several counties. A seven-member Board of Trustees governs the district, representing seven trustee areas. In the 2014–2015 academic year, total district enrollment was 22,000 students, and the estimated Full-Time Equivalent Students (FTES) is 37,110. The total operating budget for the district in 2015–2016 was over $375 million.

## Fletcher Community College

The college provides the advantages of a medium-sized community college campus in a friendly and contemporary setting, serving more than 8,020 students from the Riley and Raven communities with various higher education learning opportunities. FCC provides a broad, technology-based curriculum that meets its clients' individual educational needs in a global environment. FCC is known for its pioneering spirit and favorable climate. The staff and leadership have created a college that is innovative, responsive, respectful, collegial, and focused on student success. In the 2005 fall semester, the college opened a 100,000-square-foot Academic Center (AC) that includes a state-of-the-art computer lab, classroom facilities, art studio, bookstore, multimedia studio, physics science laboratories, assembly hall, and distance learning center. In Phase II of the FCC site, which opened in January 2010, an additional 90,000-square-foot AC houses allied health and science laboratories, a fitness center, dance studio, library/learning center, student services, offices, and classrooms. The campus also has a bookstore and internet café for student and staff convenience. The college has the Jack Community College and Hedge Campus, located approximately five miles away from the main campus to provide additional classroom space.

Many students attend FCC to fulfill their general education requirements or prepare for transfer to four-year institutions. In addition to the transfer function, career technical programs leading to certificates and associate degrees reflecting the most current job skills and knowledge have been established. High demand occupational programs include criminology, child development, business, computer/information systems, and multimedia/graphics. A $10 million licensed childcare facility is available on the new college campus for high school and college students taking child development and pre-teaching courses. Funding was secured to construct the state-of-the-art Early Childhood Education Center through collaboration with the State, Sparks Unified School District, and Red Moon Community College District.

## FLETCHER COMMUNITY COLLEGE STATEMENT

FCC is the college of choice for academic excellence, innovation, and student achievement. Our multifaceted approach, including, but not limited to, student contact, technological outreach, and building community partnerships, will provide a comprehensive system of learning opportunities and educational support services.

### Fletcher Community College Vision: One Student at a Time

We believe education is based on integrity, generosity, and accountability.

We foster critical, creative, and engaged thinking.

We support student success by preparing students for their futures and the community's future through career/technical certificates, degrees, and transfer programs.

We cultivate community partnerships to enhance student learning and success.

We engage in a reflective, data-driven cycle of research and innovation focused on learning and student outcomes.

We embrace diversity and serve all students of the community.

### Opportunities and Challenges

The new college president of FCC will:

1. Foster the continuance of a lively college climate based on collegiality, mutual trust and respect, and participatory governance.
2. Inspire, encourage, and empower college staff and faculty to provide excellent programs and services that lead to student success and completion.
3. Ensure a college climate that values diversity in its students and staff and promotes cultural proficiency.
4. Expand the college's career and technical education programs and offerings.
5. Lead the college's efforts to create and follow a comprehensive strategic plan based on a widely accepted view of its future.
6. Acquire revenue from nontraditional sources and carefully allocate fiscal resources, including practicing effective enrollment management.
7. Partner with business and industry, local education, and other governmental and nonprofit agencies to meet the community's needs.

8. Be a strong advocate for FCC, while also maintaining positive working relationships with colleagues at other colleges throughout the District that include Alpha, Beta, Sigma Chi, and Rho and the district office.
9. Honor and support what is working well at FCC while leading the change that will be necessary as it develops and grows and creates its own identity.

## Preferred Personal and Professional Characteristics

1. Evidence of a commitment to teaching/learning and the vision of a learning-centered institution and community.
2. Knowledgeable of accreditation standards and practices.
3. Superb communication skills, including active listening.
4. A cheerleader who excels at building and maintaining a team spirit.
5. Successful experience in a multiethnic environment.
6. Skilled at meeting the needs of both traditional and nontraditional students.
7. Visible, accessible, and approachable on campus and in the community.
8. Active with students and supportive of building a climate that encourages student engagement.
9. Known for honesty, integrity, caring, and encouragement.
10. Evidence of decisive leadership and the ability to be flexible.
11. Experience in implementing innovative, thoughtful, flexible, and inclusive initiatives of the faculty.
12. Practice effective fiscal and enrollment management.
13. An entrepreneur who acquires nontraditional resources for the college.
14. Successful experience as a leader in the use of technology to facilitate learning.
15. Commitment to and knowledge of the community and economic development.
16. An influential team member of the Chancellor's Cabinet.
17. An optimist who has a sense of humor and enjoys their role in supporting the college's mission.

## Minimum Qualifications

1. An earned master's degree from an accredited higher education institution.
2. Successful senior administrative-level experience in progressively responsible, reasonably related executive positions.

3. Demonstrate a strong record of achievement that includes administrative experience in educational institutions, business, industry, government, and nonprofit organizations.
4. Demonstrated sensitivity to and understanding of the diverse academic, socioeconomic, cultural, disability, gender identity, sexual orientation, and ethnic backgrounds of community college students.

## Preferred Qualifications

1. An earned doctorate from an accredited higher education institution.
2. Senior administrative leadership experience in higher education.
3. Teaching/counseling experience in higher education.

## Essential Functions of the Position

Under administrative direction of the Chancellor and per provisions of the Education Code, the rules and regulations of the Board of Directors for Community Colleges, and the policies and administrative regulations of the District, the college president of FCC performs the following duties:

1. Serves as the chief executive officer of FCC.
2. Leads the development of the college's strategic plan and evaluation of the achievement of the college's goals and objectives.
3. Advocates for the college using a collaborative, collegial leadership style that supports the District's strategic plan and achievement of District-wide goals and objectives.
4. Develops and utilizes procedures to effectively allocate the college resources to optimize its goals and objectives.
5. Establishes and implements procedures that enhance the college's administrative and governance processes and community college center-wide communications.
6. Leads the evaluation of the college programs and services and ensures the use of research and evaluation data in institutional planning.
7. Leads, in collaboration with the college staff assistance, improvements in the college's programs and services.
8. Leads the college, in collaboration with the college staff's assistance, the development of the educational specifications for facilities required to support the college's programs.
9. Ensures adherence to the institutional accreditation policies, standards, and eligibility requirements.
10. Leads the college budget development and ensures management of the college's financial affairs in conformity with district fiscal policies and procedures.

11. Encourages and supports the development of the college's public relations, service to the community, and student outreach.
12. Promotes articulation among the college and other K-12 schools, colleges, and universities – both locally and nationally.
13. Approves all job assignments, duties, and responsibilities of academic and classified personnel.
14. Chairs the President's cabinet, participates as a member of the Chancellor's cabinet, and participates in the Board of Trustees' meeting.
15. Keeps the Chancellor informed of the college's programs and services and the community college center's needs and accomplishments.
16. Represents the college at meetings of appropriate educational agencies and organizations.
17. Ensures the college's compliance with federal, state, and district policies on equal employment opportunities and shall endeavor to protect students, employees, and community members from all discrimination, including sexual harassment.
18. Ensures that all employees work within the duties and responsibilities described in class specifications and follow all policies, rules, regulations, bargaining agreements, and procedures of the state and the district, including the requirement that access to privileged information is carefully protected.

## APPLICATION PROCEDURE

For consideration in the selection process, all interested candidates must submit the following by 5:00 p.m. on Thursday, March 24, 2020, by using the Online System and click: Fletcher President Community College.com:

1. Letter of interest, no more than five (5) pages, addresses the opportunities and challenges, preferred personal and professional characteristics, and essential functions of the position as detailed in the announcement.
2. A current resume of professional work experience, educational background, and all other pertinent information.
3. A list of names, home and business telephone numbers, and email addresses of eight references: three supervisors, two direct reports, and three faculty members from current or former institutions.

The new college president will be expected to assume duties on or about July 1, 2020. The ABC Group is conducting the search for Red Moon Community College District. For confidential inquiry, contact Dr. John Henry at Halifax Broadhouse at 838-987-8765.

## SALARY AND BENEFITS

Red Moon Community College District offers a comprehensive fringe benefit package, including medical, dental, vision, life insurance, sick leave, vacation benefits, and participation in the Red Moon Teachers Retirement System. Salary and other benefits are highly competitive, negotiable, and dependent upon experience and qualifications. Red Moon Community College District is an equal opportunity employer. It provides all persons with equal employment and educational opportunities without regard to race, ethnicity, national origin, gender, age, disability, medical condition, marital status, religion, or other factors as defined by law. The District is a Title X employer.

## READING THE JOB ANNOUNCEMENT: CRITICALLY ANALYZING THE CONTEXT

The beginning of the job announcement gives the candidate important information regarding the college or district's geography. The population's size and demographic makeup, various amenities around and outside the community are standard features. It is essential because it reveals, among other things, the kind of community one is likely to serve, the lifestyle that exists, and the amenities that could influence the decision to take the job if offered. It is to be read and digested carefully and more than once.

Generally, community college policy statements define who the organization is and how it wishes to be perceived by their constituents locally, nationally, and internationally. The policy statements address such topics as excellence, innovation, and student access and success. The college's vision is its identity pillar and explains its past, present, and future. The candidate can see the college's values and desire to be a relevant force in its community development. The college policy statements are important as they explain what exists and shape the applicant's focus related to their vision and intent.

Colleges invest a significant amount of time in defining the needs of their internal and external communities. The essential functions identified in the announcement reveal what a district expects of its CEO. It is wise when reading it to determine if one's background and skill sets are sufficient to manage the requirements. The CEO's evaluation is closely related to essential functions and greatly influences their tenure in the job. While everything listed is not possible at once, all is doable and expected by the decision-makers.

Preferred qualifications are what boards of trustees want in a candidate. It is used to create a hierarchical structure related to screening to determine who is invited or not. In deciding to apply for a CEO position, it is advisable to meet or exceed the preferred qualifications. However, having the preferred qualifications is not a single factor in the selection process, though an important one because the competition is likely to meet or exceed the standards. Minimum qualifications are essential and can get one an invitation to compete, although it is a steep climb in today's market. Many candidates have ascended to the presidency without meeting the preferred qualifications. Frequently, these people are exceptional and appear in the right place at the right time. Nevertheless, the odds favor those who meet the preferred standards.

Aspirations of the district are telegraphed in the section in the job description labeled Opportunities and Challenges. It suggests understanding some of the challenges associated with getting them to where the college wants to be. Candidates should scrutinize this section very carefully for clues. Gathering pertinent information on the college, the district, the community, and the inner workings are well worth the candidate's time. For example, one could assess the college's strengths, weaknesses, and opportunities beyond what is published. Gathering such information is useful in the interview to demonstrate advanced interest and depth of understanding of the colleges' needs.

Much of the role of the president is about the human factor (Boggs & McPhail, 2016). It revolves around communicating with others in a humane and just manner while professionally providing leadership and direction. Colleges are littered with presidents with excellent technical skills but abominable human relations skills and vice versa. It is significant to be known for honesty, integrity, caring, encouragement, and support of others. These have always been vital factors in the final discussion related to who should be selected for the job and blends quite well with experience in implementing innovative, thoughtful, flexible decisions inclusive of the internal and external communities. The title does not make one a president. It is a combination of professional skills and humane behavior and how they blend in executing the role. Anyone without this balance is likely to meet with difficulties.

The application procedures should be followed to the letter if there is an expectation to have it taken seriously. Time is of the utmost importance to faculty, staff, students, and community members who volunteer to participate in the search process and screen applications. Thus, procedures not followed by the candidates cause delays, reflect poorly on their application, and sends the wrong signal.

In this age of scarce talent, salaries are negotiable, and one should be clear about their value and expect to be monetarily rewarded accordingly.

However, make sure to know the offering salaries in the area and across the state as a guide. Nevertheless one should not diminish their value by taking a job below the market price unless planning to make a quick move upward. Herein the cover letter should adjust the resume to address one's applicable qualifications. It is especially important to write a cover letter and a resume that addresses the description specifically (Pierce, 2009).

Finally, Candidates should resist applying for the position as a test run or as an opportunity to gain experience in the interviewing process. They should avoid responding to phone calls from search firms without asking well-planned and thought-out questions based on their research of the opportunity. Above all, one image is shared in public because their persona and yours are highly respected and valued.

## REFERENCES

Boggs, G. R., & McPhail, C. J. (2016). *Practical leadership in community colleges: Navigating today's challenges.* John Wiley and Sons/Jossey-Bass.

Burrus, J., Jackson, T., Xi, N., & Steinberg, J. (2013). *Identifying the most important 21st-century workforce competencies: An analysis of the Occupational Information Network (O*NET) (ETS RR-13–21).* Educational Testing.

Pierce, S. R. (2009). How candidates can stand out in an effective way. https://www.insidehighered.com/advice/2009/05/13/how-candidates-can-stand-out-good-way.

Rios, J. A., Ling, G., Pugh, R., Becker, D., & Bacall, A. (2020). Identifying critical 21st century skills for workplace success: A content analysis of job advertisements. *Educational Researcher*, 49(2), 80–89.

Chapter Ten

# Job Announcement Description and Analysis

Steps that best prepare candidates for the interview process are explored in this chapter to help aspiring candidates explore the integral aspects of these activities.

## READ THE JOB ANNOUNCEMENT

The president's job description is significantly influenced by ongoing research on the qualifications and skills needed to perform the job. It is also guided by associations working with sitting and past presidents and boards to provide guidelines on the skills and competencies needed to perform the job. The confluence of these activities helps to shape how colleges form the content of the job description. It is linked to the institution's real and perceived needs and is influenced by hiring guidelines related historically to Affirmative Action and Title IX.

Aspirants should carefully study the job announcement because it is a resource for understanding what is expected. It defines the preparation needed to do the job. Individuals would do well to not second guess or overthink the intent of the announcement. Instead, time is better spent on preparatory work and a clear understanding of possessed competencies. It includes examining one's skill set, gathering information on the college, on the district, and on the community. Candidates should learn about the inner workings at the institution discreetly and professionally. They should talk to people (inside and outside) to determine the environment and the college's issues. Assess the strengths, weaknesses, and opportunities at the college and across the district. Repeatedly, candidates should resist applying for the position as a test run or as an opportunity to gain experience in the interviewing process. Again, candidates should avoid responding to phone calls from search firms without asking well-planned and thought-out questions based on their research of the opportunity.

## UNDERSTAND THE INSTITUTIONAL STEPS TO THE INTERVIEW

Each college prepares for the position announcement differently, although many activities involved remain standard. The creation of the job announcement begins with the Board of Trustees declaring a vacancy. It is an official interest to hire a new president. The Board strengthens that interest by gathering the insights and views of different stakeholders within the organization and throughout the community, paying attention to what they say about their concerns, needs, interests, and challenges. Such groups typically consist of the faculty, students, classified staff, community, and business groups.

The college then creates a hiring committee representing various constituent groups across the campus and from the community who volunteer their time. The hiring committee usually is a Board-approved selection committee consisting of 12–20 people of varying constituent groups. Members are recruited, scheduled, and approved according to college or district policies. Members are also exposed to Equal Employment Opportunity Commission hiring guidelines, college policy, liability, function, roles, and expectations generally. The creation of this committee is time-consuming and political.

The committee receives technical support from the district's Human Relations Department, which manages and coordinates the process and sometimes the retained search firm. The districts' Human Resources Department generally assists the committee in designing the announcement approved by the Board. Concurrent with the announcement preparation, the committee establishes the timelines for the hiring process, including dates for receiving applications, screening applicants for the interview, informing the applicants of their status, and other timelines leading to the final hiring authority. The final description that details duties, responsibilities, required qualifications, and reporting relationships are put in a deliverable form for review by a hiring committee. Typically, within 30–45 days, the job is announced in such publications as the *Chronicle of Higher Education*, Inside Higher Education, association electronic job boards, and affiliated organizations representing traditionally disadvantaged groups and women.

The search committee then convenes under the district office of Human Resources or a designee to discuss the limitations of their role, the responsibility, liability, and process, and then construct relevant questions while paying attention to information on diversity and committee biases. The committee constructs interview questions using input from constituent groups, information included in the job announcement, and feedback from the community. They also use this information to determine what tools/instruments will measure the applicants' qualifications. In many cases, after the committee makes its final recommendations, technically, they have met the Board's charge and are formally dismissed.

## Board Challenges

There are noted challenges in the Board's involvement in the creation of the job announcement. Often, members lack an understanding of the marketplace for a president. They can get bogged down in what they individually want to see in the new president, thinking it is right because it is what they and their constituents want. Based on my experience as a Chief Executive Officer Search Consultant for over a decade, a few influential individuals from special interest groups, faculty, community members, or the Board members themselves can influence announcements' content. Frequently, a personal agenda is pursued. It is generally issue-oriented and void of any real understanding of the role and function of a president.

At times, boards find themselves at odds with their fellow members because each is being politicked. They negotiate with each other, serving as proxies for their constituencies' concerns and expectations as they should. However, in excess, it is overwhelming and frequently misses commonly accepted skill sets for a president. Even though some boards take the time to organize focus groups to gather input, even those committees are put together to represent the special interests. As a result, there is a variance in specificity and content and little consensus on a current skill set desired in a community college president. Thus, districts and sometimes search firms are tasked with developing descriptions that approximate their needs, interests, and demands. The discussion within these groups mostly centers around the idea of a perfect candidate, which has never existed. Even with help from a search consultant, the finalized job description sometimes includes a long and cumbersome set of requirements that sends most candidates into a tailspin as they try to understand what is being asked and why.

To change, boards will have to do a better job in knowing and understanding the presidency's competencies, the primary performance expectations, and avoiding overloading a checklist of presidential responsibilities that make it impossible for a president after getting the job to be successful. They need to work in harmony with the American Association of Community Colleges and leading associations, who are actively training presidents and undergo the American Association of Community Colleges Trustee association training programs. They need to focus on concretely building their case via the job description for why their job is the ideal place for a candidate in search of a presidency. Boggs and McPhail (2016) give informed counsel when they write that community college boards are responsible for the institution's current and future vitality to ensure that the college or district is operated effectively, efficiently, and ethically. It is a weighty impressive responsibility that requires expert management by Boards of Trustees.

## Screening and Interviews Processes

After the job announcement is publicized, candidates are screened by the committee. They then are recommended to compete in what is typically called the "second round." At this juncture, the committee asks a set of pre-approved adopted questions. Final candidates are invited back to make presentations at an open forum, and it could take all day. Candidates meet with constituent groups and members of the lay, professional, and business communities to answer general and sometimes specific questions. Each constituent group is permitted a one hour question and answer session. The answers are collected and used by the hiring manager as part of the decision-making process. The committee may include members of the hiring manager's selected team, including the former President, members of the Board, or some other vetting specific to the college's norms and policies.

Committees usually display common professional courtesies to candidates on the day of the interview and throughout the entire process. The candidate is welcomed, followed by the protocols that include an overview of the interview process. The place and location are planned to be inviting, comfortable, and private with no interruptions. Consistent interviewing formats, i.e., in-person, phone, or virtual meetings, are practiced and consistent to ensure an equitable and fair process. Such actions ensure that each candidate is allotted the same amount of time and in the same format. The hiring criterion listed on the committee's rating sheet is likely linked to one or more interview questions. Specialized or specific skills and abilities typically are assessed and measured for reporting on the candidates. The criterion set for selection varies from place to place, state to state, college to college, and should be considered by applicants when applying. States like California and Washington clearly define the required minimum and preferred qualifications. It is a big piece of their screening process and is so stated in the job announcement. Hiring committee members are given access to the hiring pool and must review the applications over a previously established period.

Based on prior approval by the candidate, the reference checks commence for finalists. It involves verification of the accuracy of the candidate's representation of facts. It is a full process and is not limited just to the references provided by the applicant. It encompasses talking with past and present peers on various levels. It can and does extend to contacting service clubs, community groups, and reviewing social media profiles. Newspaper stories and activities associated with the candidate as a person, including any legal infractions, domestic violence or abuse, tax issues, and bankruptcy, are always of interest. It is wise for candidates to appropriately inform their boss of where they are in the process to avoid any surprises.

### Final Meeting

After completing interviews, forums, and reference checks, the finalists are invited to a formal meeting with the CEO and perhaps a representative from the Board. The meeting could last from one to two hours, guided by a series of structured questions specific to the interviewers. Candidates are usually asked to relax. They are encouraged to engage in an open and candid conversation, according to the Board and the hiring manager's interests and concerns. Decision-makers in the room tend to slant on the college and district, its needs, and the candidate's fit to serve those needs. For them, the pressure associated with the margin for error is exceedingly high. Unless the hiring agency is interested in visiting the candidate's campus, the district may make an offer within two to three days following the interview. At this point, the candidate has several decisions to make, and they include, among other things, accepting an offer, negotiating a fair and competitive salary and fringe benefits package, confirming working conditions, starting date, and the timeline for exiting the current job, which should be managed very delicately.

## PREPARE FOR THE INTERVIEW

It is common for candidates to spend a considerable amount of time mounting self-imposed fear and dread regarding the search committee, who their competition might be, and who the inside candidate is. Much of this can be managed and certainly eliminated. Pierce (2009) correctly points out that candidates in all searches are inevitably confronted with variables that they cannot control, most notably the competition's strength and the chemistry between each candidate and the hiring committee. Pierce explains that it is common for search committee members to believe that their pool contains several people who could effectively fill the position and find themselves drawn, especially to only one of them. As an experienced president, community college careerist, and CEO executive search consultant, it is contended that candidates can take positive steps to enhance their chances for success. They can also influence how they are received, even though they may not end up being a finalist.

## Pay Strict Attention to the Cover Letter

Committee members pay attention to well-written, engaging, and even inspiring letters in which candidates describe in compelling terms how their experience and credentials translate to the position being sought. The most important thing is to have a unique letter for each application filed. It means avoiding stock letters with the following format: beginning and ending with a paragraph that mentions the hiring institution's name, but in the body of the letter, focus exclusively on their self-perceived strengths and accomplishments without regard to the college, and end with a repeat of how much they want the position. Similarly, never use a generic letter that starts with "To Whom It May Concern." That said, there are key points to include: (a) story about why there is an interest in the institution, (b) purpose for applying at this moment in their career, and (c) why they would be an effective president at this time in leading the college. Letters should document what it is in your background that would appeal to the search committee. For instance, if the college wants its next president to have the capacity to be a successful fundraiser, then highlight relevant experiences. They could include such a role in passing a bond measure, writing grant proposals, participating in the cultivation of gifts, speaking to the alumni, prospective students, and community groups on behalf of the institution. It is always useful to reference those who know about one's role in these areas. Finally, the letter should include specific, direct connections to the college, including mission and information gleaned from the website or the academic and classified senates' minutes. Candidates should have a clear understanding of the college's history, including union issues in the district, about the college/district budget. They can obtain considerable insight into the district by talking to students, reading college publications, current and back issues of local newspapers, meeting with leaders from various social clubs, and perchance talking to the outgoing leader before officially applying, and finally, personally visiting the campus to sense its rhythm and flow.

### Avoid Unforgiveable Missteps

Edit the cover letter and application to avoid sending in the paperwork that references another institution other than the intended college. Such an approach suggests a lack of care and respect for the college's process. It communicates an all-purpose letter that the candidate has likely prepared in response to other ads. Always edit for grammar and flow. Above all, avoid sloppiness in the paperwork in terms of writing and delivery. Finally, make sure the resume and cover letter include the correct phone number and email address for you and the references.

### Tailor the Resume

A tightly constructed resume will get the committee's attention because it will clearly show the candidate's breadth and depth and potential fit for the college. Remember that the resume should not restate the information in the cover letter. Avoid submitting a lengthy resume because committees will most likely dismiss it. As a presidential candidate, do not provide a detailed list of everything accomplished. Instead, select targeted items that address the announcement and list them under headings like Doctoral education (where, date of completion, and area focus), Positions held (listing most current first), Grants, Publications, Presentations, Committee Membership, and Professional Accomplishments. While some candidates do not want to put dates due to age discrimination, this only distracts the committee as they try to speculate and calculate the date. Be proud of the journey and the time it took to get there. If the college wants the expertise presented, age will not matter. Take note and feel assured that committees are willing to look at candidates regardless of their age, as there is a trend showing that Boards are hiring those 65 or older and hiring some in the mid-to-late 30s.

### Devote Time to the References

Presidential candidates should think carefully about identifying people who can support their candidacy factually and truthfully. Include not only faculty members and senior administrators, but also some Board members with whom the candidate has worked. Including the name of friends or prominent people who know little of one's work experience or have supervised one's work is of little value to the screening committee. Do not list names beyond what is called for in the application. One should alert references that a call may be coming to them from an agency applied too. References should be provided with a brief description of one's resume, the job, and ideas on why the job excites the interest.

### Demonstrate Honesty and Integrity in the Interview

Do not shy away from addressing any issues that might be of concern to the committee. Committees appreciate honesty and transparency. For instance, explanations as to why one is making a career change, particularly after only having served in an institution for two years or less, is of interest and importance. Equally important is an explanation for a downward or lateral move for two years or more in the journey. Also, do not be afraid to address personal issues involving accusations or negative media coverage honestly. Life happens, and never be afraid to be transparent. It is better to be judged upfront than later to be told something was uncovered that was not revealed in the process, and that is unfavorable. It is a slippery slope, and one can easily be tempted to wait until you are asked. However, this only delays the inevitable and will cast suspicion on one's integrity and ethics. Other areas of interest are dressing appropriately for the institution, showing the energy of interest during the interview, not being pretentious, and using effectively nonverbal communication commands.

### Communicate a Genuine, Honest Interest in the College

Hiring committees know when a candidate is shopping or getting an interview experience for the next job. Serious candidates appear at the interview confident and prepared to engage the committee on what they know and feel about the institution. They can articulate the strengths and promises of the institution and are honest in their assessments. They ask the right questions and are apt to provide thoughtful responses to questions being asked. Before accepting an invitation to an interview, come to terms with such critical questions: Do I honestly want this job? Am I prepared to take a cut in salary? Am I willing to live in the community? Am I prepared to send the kids to local schools? Am I willing to have my spouse or significant other quit a current job and seek one in the community where the college is located? Finally, am I sure that I want to do the work that the position requires?

## REFERENCES

Boggs, G. R., & McPhail, C. J. (2016). *Practical leadership in community colleges: Navigating today's challenges*. John Wiley and Sons/Jossey-Bassey.

Pierce, S. R. (2009). How candidates can stand out in an effective way. https://www.insidehighered.com/advice/2009/05/13/how-candidates-can-stand-out-good-way.

Part III

# Stories from the Field

Chapter Eleven

# Lived Experiences of California Community College Buttimer Recipients

This chapter examines selected California community college presidents who were awarded the Buttimer award for leadership excellence.

## BUTTIMER AWARD

The Harry Buttimer Distinguished Award (ACCCA) is the Association of California Community College Administrators' (ACCCA, 2020) oldest and most prestigious leadership award. Named for the late Harry Buttimer, the award was initiated in 1986 and symbolized the qualities he was known for, including integrity, compassion, strength in leadership, contributions to colleagues and the profession, and contributions to the college district community. As a founding member of ACCCA and its first Legislative Commission Chairperson, Harry Buttimer's contributions helped establish the Association as a stakeholder in community college finance and legislation, which helped set the foundation for programs and services used by members today. Each year, one or more sitting California community college presidents are awarded the Buttimer Award.

This chapter profiles 41 former Buttimer Award recipients. Table 11.1 profiles the demographics showing 30 males and 11 female participants. Fifty-nine percent of the participants were White males. Those with doctoral degrees were typically the more recent awardees. Of the 28 participants who earned the award within the past 15 years, 73.1% had a doctoral degree. Awardees before 2005 mostly had master's degrees while two had a nontraditional degree of Certified Public Accountant and Juris Doctorate. Ninety percent of doctorate holders stayed in their CEO positions for ten years or more, and 67% of master's degree holders occupied CEO positions for ten years or more.

## ASCENDENCY PREPARATIONS

The Buttimer awardees identified four steps that they took to prepare themselves for a pathway to the presidency. Most indicated they were very well prepared for their job, while only a few indicated they were moderately prepared.

### Mentorship

Among the Buttimer Award recipients, 92.5% of those with doctorate degrees and 42.86% of those with master's degrees had formal and informal mentorship from supervisors, presidents, and respected friends. The most recent awardees all agreed that being formally mentored is a crucial step to becoming and eventually being an active CEO. Even those who did not have mentors noted that a "good mentor could be a useful relationship to expand knowledge and skills and to have a confidant to help accelerate progress in generating credibility and trust among staff and trustees."

### Worked at the Same College/District

Most of the Buttimer recipients worked at the same community college for 3–18 years before their selection as a president. Most identified the extended tenure at the same institution as a primary and a significant benefit because it enabled familiarity with institutional culture, policies, and practices. One awardee noted that "familiarity builds when mentors are from the same institution." For awardees who did not have mentors, their extended tenure at a community college was the most important criteria for building their professional goals.

### Leadership Development Program Participation

All Buttimer award recipients shared that an essential step in their preparation for the presidency was their participation in developmental programs sponsored by professional associations at local, state, and national levels. Each president mentioned that a critical outcome of their participation was the immediate improvement of their skill sets. Many also mentioned that participation in these leadership development programs led to relevant mentoring and networking opportunities. One typical response was that these programs "help you learn as much as possible and prove valuable, if not essential, to selecting options for accomplishing changes needed to improve the performance of the institution you aspire to lead." Another recipient noted that these programs "accelerate your skill-building by receiving leadership lessons from some of the best leaders available and building a network of smart and experienced colleagues who help you understand the complexities of various types of institutions and CEO positions."

### Obtain Specific Skills

The Buttimer awardees identified four skills they felt were necessary for their ascendancy preparation.

### Become an Expert

The skill of gathering information, understanding research, and assessing the validity of that research was mentioned by all Buttimer awardees as necessary skills to build expertise. Being an expert was noted as necessary because it enabled the awardee to use knowledge to advance their vision. Another reason for building expertise was, as one recipient said, being an "expert allowed me to know how my skills could best benefit the institution."

### Problem Solving

Problem-solving was another skill that was honored by the awardees. Identifying the problem was as important as the skill to see the problem as an opportunity. These skills were identified as a fundamental one to building relationships and moving the vision into action. The latter being a primary designator of a transformative leader. The process of problem-solving in terms of ascendancy preparation included, as one recipient noted, the ability to "know when to problem-solve alone and when to invite others into the problem-solving process."

### Networking

Networking was identified as an essential skill that involved building and maintaining action forward connections between people. The Buttimer awardees shared a need to network and a critical need to learn how to network effectively. One president shared that this process "meant not to be a passive leader." Aligned with the skill of networking is to know how to use it effectively. One awardee shared the importance of "learning how to work with and through people, and to give credit to others for their accomplishments."

### Introspection

Awardees applied the skill of introspection into two components. The first aimed to frame the importance of life-long learning. In this context, the skill of always questioning and wanting to learn more, especially as it relates to personal self-growth, is what many of the Buttimer awardees said sustained their effective leadership. One president provided an example that linked preparation to:

> adhering to the Rotary four-way test of the things we think, say, or do: Is it the truth? Is it fair to all concerned? Will it build goodwill and better friendships? Will it be Beneficial to all concerned? The second component framed around finding one's voice and learning about self, developing a vision of leadership that one can live by every day.

The second framed around finding one's voice, learning about self, and developing a vision of leadership that you can live by every day.

## REFLECTIONS ON WHAT IT TAKES FOR SUCCESS

The Buttimer award recipients reflected on three categories of what it took for them to be successful in the presidential position:

### Context

The Buttimer award recipients noted that being aware of trends, relationships, and changing educational needs was crucial in getting the job. They included knowing the trends taking place in postsecondary education at the time, the factors that influenced the trends, and the working knowledge of how other presidents at various institutions were responding to those trends. One Buttimer awardee shared that knowing context also allows the potential leader to "effectively build relationships with other experienced CEOs through mentoring, on networking, and collaboration." Finally, Buttimer awardees talked about how context extended to knowledge about the institution itself, focusing on its sociopolitical and economic needs and the range of people in the institution. The focus of gaining institutional context was to "understand the institution's complexity of values and skills." Knowing the context is also related to learning and relearning to be better informed and able to interpret the positions of employees and trustees correctly.

## Vision

The Buttimer award recipients noted the importance of having a forward-thinking vision with a defined set of goals for themselves, their career trajectory, and for what they wanted to support community college education. Having a vision was necessary to motivate all leadership team members to feel free to share their various viewpoints and share the community's historical knowledge being served by the college. An articulated vision was also seen as essential for enabling others to agree to adopt their comprehensive strategies. One president said that "vision, when articulated well, helps members accept proportional responsibility for implementing and documenting various aspects of the strategy adopted." Simultaneously, other presidents mentioned the importance of retaining "an open mind so that the vision can continuously evolve as a result of self-learning and improvement to be better prepared to make informed decisions, accelerate problem-solving, and receive mentorship from experienced professionals with whom they network." Finally, all of the Buttimer awardees agreed that vision was needed to work harmoniously with personal passions.

## Motivations

The Buttimer awardees were asked to select a word that best describes what motivated them to persist in their journey to a community college CEO. Figure 11.1 shows the word mapping of these words. The awardees' words included being creative, caring, having patience, focusing, and having passion.

Figure 11.1 Word mapping: Buttimer awardee motivations.

## CHALLENGES AND STRATEGIES USED TO OVERCOME CHALLENGES WHILE IN THE JOB

The Buttimer award recipients were asked about the most significant challenges they encountered as a first-time community college CEO.

### Time

The greatest challenge mentioned by each Buttimer awardee was time. The concept of time, however, had various meanings that included (a) time to learn what their job requirements were and then having the time to do everything they learned; (b) finding the time to do what they wanted that would allow them to realize their vision; (c) having lots of things to do but only limited time to do it; and (d) balancing their workload with their family life.

### Personal Level Challenges

Four personal challenges were shared by many of the Buttimer recipients. The first challenge was the need to continually strive to build respect and support from faculty and other staff. It was especially crucial for the presidents who began at the same college and who already had relations with faculty and staff, and then were surprised when they found difficulties in "transitioning from serving in a single segment of college operations, such as student support services, to the president position." A second challenge was the need to continually reflect and introspect on how one's personality affected one's leadership style. One awardee said that "not being a people person and not having a soft side, which stemmed from my earlier training as a marine, was a constant challenge that I simply just had to learn." A third challenge was identifying others as collaborators to help reach a shared institutional vision. Most said they did this by building a collaborative team that would work together to "reach/achieve consensus-oriented goals involving the entire faculty, staff, student body, and community leaders in developing missions, goals, objectives, and timelines for the college/district." Finally, several Buttimer recipients noted that they found it challenging to work with staff to reduce or remove bias against them serving as a president based on their gender, race/ethnicity, and youth. Such biases were mentioned as an unforeseen challenge, and as one president said, "the shock took me by surprise and impacted many of the decisions that I made in the first year." Many respondents indicated that by experiencing personal challenges, they learned to have a passion for continuous learning to make informed decisions and train staff in negotiating skills to promote effective teamwork.

## Institutional Level Challenges

Most of the Buttimer awardees expressed satisfaction and some even exhilaration about their ability to improve the college's performance. The presidents identified via four broad institutional challenges what they felt would help future presidents be effective change agents: team building to embrace their visions for the college, financial solvency, building positive relationships with the community served by the college(s), and student learning outcomes. Of most importance was the ability to overcome targeted institutional challenges.

## Budget Issues Challenges

All the respondents mentioned budget-related challenges, especially the challenge of dealing with chronic underfunding and how it negatively influenced college programs and outreach – a central topic related to budget issues was keeping the college's financial condition healthy. One president said it was a challenge to "rebuild trust between administrators and faculty where severe budget deficits had been encountered before their selection as the CEO." Another noted the importance of "maintaining positive employer/employee relations when resources are insufficient, and while everyone is trying to keep their specific programs alive." Another president reported not being familiar with funding formulas, which quickly forced a situation to learn because of the college's particular importance. Thus, not only did they need to learn new skills quickly, but they quickly needed to learn to be useful and effective in the process. Finally, the Buttimer awardees emphasized learning to effectively manage and mitigate conflicts with employee groups and citizens residing in the community served by the college. Several awardees mentioned that they needed to learn about political influences on their college resources and then use that knowledge to manage human and fiscal resources to promote college goals and promote employees' and trustees' professional development. Funding challenges have a direct connection to the economic and political choices made in the state of California in the 1980s. Even though Proposition 13 was passed in 1978, long before any of the presidents gained their positions, it still influenced all college decisions.

## Collective Bargaining Challenges

As seen through the Buttimer recipients' lens, collective bargaining is an essential tool, but it presented various challenges. All the awardees noted the difficulties in having different sides reach consensus. One recipient said that "working with shared governance policy in California to promote connectivity meant dealing with unions, union mentality, and sometimes viciousness of behavior among union members and leaders." Another mentioned the challenges of:

> dealing with collective bargaining within the fiscal impact of Proposition 13 that made it difficult as I tried to accomplish the objective of building a new campus for the district and the need to consider faculty layoffs as part of a strategy to balance the budget of the college.

## Management Challenges

Many of the Buttimer awardees mentioned the need to build positive working relations with the college's upper-level management staff and become familiar with the board of trustee members' strengths and weaknesses. While most mentioned that they use team building to be successful, some shared that building teams "are a challenge but done successfully sets the foundation for success." For example, one president mentioned how "important it is to know to build the *right team*, that was inclusive of the entire college population, including locally elected trustees." Each of the Buttimer awardees used various terminologies when speaking about the need to build strong collaborative teams, although some less favorable than others, but each attributed a solid team as helping them to develop consensus around vision and future goals and then to have these stakeholders embrace being held accountable for their own tasks in achieving institutional goals. As one president said:

> the consensus team building also generated mentality among college leaders to be mutually supportive and solution-oriented as challenges and obstacles are encountered. The creation of collaborative teams also contributed to inspiring productive deliberation of new ideas to improve outcomes throughout the college.

Finally, all mentioned their need to generate a typical mentality rather than using their authority as the president.

## Personnel Issues and Challenges

The Buttimer awardees defined personnel issues as knowing when and how to deal with personnel fairly and equitably. Challenges included knowing how to work lawfully on sexual harassment, racism, faculty termination, and unionism. Successful outcomes were attributed to the culmination of understanding the context of the issue/problem, using critical thinking skills to address the issue/problem, and, most importantly, knowing how to stand by one's vision in difficult times.

## Building Positive Relationships with the Community Challenges

Several of the Buttimer awardees reflected on their need to build a positive relationship with the college community. Building positive relationships was essential for one president to effectively build a new campus and upgrade the existing campus facilities. By working closely with their trustees, many of the presidents shared that they could enhance communication with the community's residents and eventually get their support for college-related projects and plans. One president noted that "a result of building a positive relationship with community residents led to their success in promoting voter approval of multimillion-dollar bonds to renovate existing college facilities and build new facilities."

## Student Learning Outcomes Challenges

All of the Buttimer awardees placed a high priority on improving student outcomes and not just effectively managing the college. Central to their success was not allowing politics or finances to distract their attention from promoting activities and services to improve student achievement. The Buttimer awardees also noted the importance of promoting faculty's professional development to build a personal contribution to student learning based on current teaching and learning models that focused on student outcomes. In reflection, the presidents talked about their need to "build my own level of expertise about curriculum and pedagogy." Connected was the need to gather and retain data on decisions that promoted positive student outcomes and tracking increases in the numbers of students graduating annually. Specifically, there was a need to expand outreach to communities with highly concentrated residents of color and to encourage their enrollment and achievement at their colleges.

## SPECIFIC STRATEGIES USED TO OVERCOME MOST DIFFICULT CHALLENGES

The Buttimer awardees listed five thematic strategies they used to overcome the most difficult challenges.

### Personal Vision

Similar to the literature, identifying and building a personal vision was seen as the most important strategy to overcome challenges. However, the Buttimer recipients all talked about the various steps involved in building their vision. One president mentioned the need to "remain an honest person." Another expressed the need to "stay healthy in body and mind so you can have the energy to do whatever is necessary to address the challenges you faced." Finally, another president mentioned the need to "have a fearless management manner and willingness to take a measured risk."

### Mentoring and Outreach

The Buttimer awardees mentioned that effectively dealing with challenges meant reaching out to others for guidance and support. One president mentioned the strategy to "maintain close interaction with former bosses and trustees to align their thoughts and objectives with my vision and goals for the college." Another president explained the need to "build relationships with other CEOs to have the advantage of an experienced mentor and to learn about multiple options for addressing similar challenges that other CEOs have encountered."

### Leadership Strategies

Each of the Buttimer awardees detailed the leadership strategies they felt helped them identify and overcome challenges. Many of these strategies were connected to personality characteristics such as one president shared to "realize that I cannot do everything that is needed to be done to improve institutional performance and to maintain a persistent focus on student outcomes." Another president shared the importance of "maintaining self-confidence in hiring good, smart people, even those who may be smarter than yourself. Recognize their expertise and engage them in strategic planning. However, to always hold people accountable for the responsibilities assigned to them."

Other strategies intersected with professionalism, such as "to remain focused on professional values and not the system of community colleges in California as a way to solicit others respect." Another president shared the importance of "building respect with employees and Board members who have different expectations and standards for you based on your racial, ethnicity, gender, or youth." Lastly, one president shared the importance of "do whatever is necessary to be an effective leader and to address difficult situations fairly."

## Communication Strategies

Communication strategies were seen to ground all leadership decisions and were listed among the most important in dealing with challenges. One president shared the importance to "listen carefully and communicate regularly with campus staff and leadership." Another president shared the need to "build trust so that others feel safe to make corrections in activities when necessary or to take ownership of quickly generating alternative solutions." Finally, a president shared the need to have "consistent communication to enhance trust in collaborating with others. It allows me to be flexible in modifying strategies to achieve the vision and goals that I have promoted for the colleges and district."

## Research

While all the Buttimer awardees talked about the importance of building expertise, the more recent awardees applied that to research and analysis skills. One president shared the importance of "constantly reviewing data and using that data to realize your vision." Another agreed about the importance of "sharing data to enhance the knowledge of employees and governing board members as a means to encourage them to adopt your vision and to generate consensus." Another talked about the importance of using "analytical research to enhance informed decision-making, so I can empower the college leadership team by sharing empirical information to enhance problem-solving and strategic planning."

## Proudest Accomplishments

Finally, many of the Buttimer awardees pointed to their decade-plus years of service in one district as a mark of consistency. Others mentioned that their proudest accomplishment was their agenda to increase the diversity of faculty, staff, and administration purposefully, which was a noted accomplishment. Another accomplishment identified by the Buttimer awardees was their impact on students' lives and, through that, their extended families and serving the needs of underrepresented students.

**Table 11.1 Profiles of Buttimer Award Recipients and Sitting Presidents**

| | | Buttimer | | Sitting Presidents | |
|---|---|---|---|---|---|
| Gender | Male | 30 | | 6 | |
| | Female | 11 | | 5 | |
| Race | | Male | Female | Male | Female |
| | White | 24 | 7 | 1 | 1 |
| | African-American | 3 | 2 | 1 | 1 |
| | Latinx | 2 | 2 | 1 | 1 |
| | Asian | 1 | | 1 | 1 |
| | Native-American | | | 1 | 1 |
| | Muslim | | | 1 | |
| Education | Recent Awardees | 28 | 73.1% had doctorate degrees | | |
| | Master's Degree | 11 | 67% had master's degree | | |
| | Doctorate Degree | 10 | 5 male and 5 female | | |

Lastly, one awardee explained that their proudest accomplishment was "when discovering you are no longer coordinated with your leadership within the organization and able to move on."

## REFERENCES

ACCCA (The Administrator's Association – California Community Colleges – Association of California Community College). (2020). https://www.accca.org/i4a/pages/index.cfm?pageid=3296.

Chapter Twelve

# Lived Experiences of Sitting Community College Presidents

This chapter explores the lived experiences of sitting community college presidents. These individuals were chosen based on the personal knowledge of some of them and national leaders' recommendations for others. These Sitting Presidents were purposefully chosen to reflect a diverse selection of racial, ethnic, and gendered individuals working today in community colleges. Also, they represented presidents who were new to their position but had been in the field for a while.

## DEMOGRAPHICS

Table 11.1 details the demographics of Sitting Presidents who participated in the study. Among them were six males and five females, two who worked in rural community colleges, one who worked on the East Coast, two in the Mid-Atlantic, two in the South, two in the West Coast, one in the Northwest, two in the Mid-West, and one in the Plains. For most, this was their first presidency. The average years of service in their current position were 5.1 years. One president was in the position for six months, five were in their position for three years or less, two were in their position for 5–11 years, and one was in the position for 17 years. Eight of the Sitting Presidents planned to retire within the next five years and gave the benchmark of 2026 as their date. Three presidents planned to retire in 2032, giving that date to indicate that retirement would "not be in the near future." The diverse profile of the Sitting Presidents was purposefully done to gain a range of opinions and experiences. Quotes are included from these presidents and refer to each by their racial or ethnic identification and gender.

The lessons learned by the Sitting Presidents align with the literature and with the narratives of the Buttimer award recipients in terms of steps taken to get to the presidency, ascendency preparation, significant challenges, and advice they would give to aspiring leaders.

## PROFESSIONAL PATHWAYS

Each of the Sitting Presidents shared insight on the steps that led to their presidency.

### Traditional and Nontraditional Pathways

Unlike the Buttimer awardees who spent considerable time at the institution where they eventually became presidents, only four of the Sitting Presidents had their pathways within their same college. Of the rest, one moved to a different college, but within the same state, while the remaining six moved to another state to gain their presidency position. While the Buttimer awardees' professional pathways were relatively uniform and considered part of a traditional leadership pathway (Wiseman & Vaughan, 1988), only three Sitting Presidents embarked on a traditional academic pathway. They started in various mid-level and senior positions at a community college before taking on its role. The rest of the sitting college presidents had unique pathways, with many of them beginning in a nontraditional pathway (Raby & Valeau, 2019), such as coming from positions as a high school teacher, a university professor, a director of a national resource center, a medical doctor, as Vice-President of a manufacturing corporation, and a member of the Tribal Council.

Nonetheless, once in the community college system, most of the Sitting Presidents then followed the traditional leadership pathway from Director to Dean to Vice-President. Four were Dean or Vice-President of Instruction, and two were Dean of Student Services, one each was a Dean of Student Life, Dean of Career and Technical Education, and Vice-President of Workforce & Continuing Education. Only two of the Sitting Presidents had no prior dean or vice-president experiences.

Two leadership pathway theories can be used to describe the trajectory of the experiences of Sitting Presidents. The intentional pathway theory shows that individuals deliberately choose to enroll by using strategic planning (Garza Mitchell & Cano-Monreal, 2015). The unintentional pathway theory shows that choices to move along a career pipeline are not always planned (Garza Mitchell & Eddy, 2008).

## Intentionality

Several of the Sitting Presidents intentionally planned to gain their presidency position. Intentionality included making several purposeful choices. One clear choice was long-term planning. One President said, "once I came to a decision . . . I began to plan how to get there, and I became intentional in getting myself ready" (Asian Male). Intentionality also involved strategically changing one job context for another; as one noted, "I had to determine if making a shift from being a researcher at comprehensive universities to the community college system would work for me. As it turned out, it was not a difficult transition" (Latinx Male). Another clear choice was a designated outreach to current Sitting Presidents to request an opportunity to "observe and consult on how they deal with difficult issues, like budget management, personnel issues, change management, fund-raising, and legislative advocacy" (African-American Male). A final example of intentionality was the purposeful enrolling in professional development programs offered by the American Association of Community Colleges or those offered by Achieving the Dream as "participating in executive training, or executive leadership coaching helps; reading up on articles on presidential transition also helps" (African-American Female). Another benefit of these development programs was knowing when one is ready. One respondent said that:

> after being sponsored by my Latina professional mentor to attend the Executive Leadership Institute (ELI) sponsored by the League for Innovation in Community College, I was able to assess my skill sets and develop the confidence necessary to begin exploring community college presidencies. (Latinx Female)

## Accidental Entry

Some of the Sitting Presidents did not intentionally plan to enter into the presidency position. It corresponds with the literature that shares not everyone wants to be president and enters the position by happenstance (Garza Mitchell & Eddy, 2008). One president shared that "I was satisfied with doing what I was doing. My professional friends had other thoughts and dragged me into the competition" (Asian Female). Another president shared that "working at the community college was not on my career map . . . as I was ascending into relatively higher corporate positions"

(Muslim Male). Nevertheless, another sitting president shared how accidental entry turned into intentionality:

> I never thought I would pursue a community college presidency until a Latina college president, who eventually became one of my professional mentors, told me that I should pursue one. She saw in me what I did not know, and that was that I possessed the capacity to be a successful president. (Latinx Male)

Moreover, one sitting president shared that:

> my ascendancy was not planned and happened by a two-step fate. The college was experiencing issues with the then president, although I had no preparation or planning to be an educator, let alone a college president, I was appointed a president. (Native-American Male)

## Persistence

The Sitting Presidents were unique in the importance that they gave to persistence in the leadership pathway context. It was a skill that the Buttimer awardees did not mention. In gaining the presidency position, many shared that ascendency does not always occur in a straight line. Many of the Sitting Presidents mentioned the importance of learning, trying, and even trying again for positions. One president shared, "I applied twice for the same position at the same institution and became successful the second time" (Asian Male). Another said that "mistakes provided an opportunity to grow and learn from your mistakes" (African-American Male). Finally, another emphasized persistence in terms of "coming up through the ranks allowed me credibility when developing relationships. Relationships are essential to success in these difficult leadership positions" (White Female).

## Professional Pathway, Lived Experiences

While it is common to have a linear pathway to the presidency, as noted, many of the Sitting Presidents also acknowledged the importance of their alternative pathways. However, of interest to this book are the variations that exist within each of the pathways.

### Traditional Academic Pathway

Story 1: "I embarked on a traditional academic pathway which included my position as a faculty to the dean of student life then executive dean of instruction and student services, and then campus provost before becoming the president" (Asian Male).

### Traditional Professional Pathway

Story 1: "I embarked on a traditional professional pathway that started with the director of institutional effectiveness, to the dean of an academic division, to vice president of academic affairs, and then to the president" (Asian Female).

### Combination of Academic and Professional Pathways

Story 1: "My pathway started as a full-time faculty and then a vocational education coordinator, and then I became a department chair and academic senate representative. Later, I became an institutional researcher, executive dean of instruction, a division dean, and then left the college to become an associate director at a national non-profit organization. Years later, I went back to college as a vice-president of instruction and then finally to the President. All of these positions were in the same state" (White Female).

### Cross-Institutional Academic Pathways

Story 1: "Cross-institutional academic pathway had me starting as a student services professional in the Educational Opportunity Program (EOP) within a State University System. Then, I became a director of the program and later the assistant vice president in student affairs in the same State University system. I then changed institutions and accepted the vice president of student services position at a community college in the same state and later became president in another state" (Latinx Male).

Story 2: "I started as an Upward Bound curriculum coordinator at a university and then changed institutional types to take a position as the associate director of admissions at a community college in the same state. Simultaneously, I took a part-time instructor position at the same community college to merge the professional and academic pathways. Eventually, I became the New College dean of business & technology, then the vice president of instruction and later the president at another community college but in the same state" (Latinx Female).

### Beginning Career in a Non-Higher Education Position

Story 1: "I began my professional career as a Catholic monk and then taught at a high school. I later became a Corporate Trainer, then a Technical Assistance Manager at a University. I transitioned to the community college and began a business faculty's traditional academic pathway to a director, dean, and then vice president for Workforce & Continuing Education. To continue on the pathway, I realized that I had to move to another state to take a vice-chancellor position and then become a president. I am currently a president in another state" (White Male).

Story 2: "I started as a K-12 faculty, and later while pursuing a medical degree, I became an adjunct community college faculty. I continued teaching at the community college while I was doing post-doctoral work in dentistry at the university. While at the university, I became a mentor at a local community college and later changed my pathway to stay at that college to become a Director and then the interim executive dean and then the permanent executive dean. The presidency position required me to move to another community college in the same state" (African-American Male).

Story 3: "I started working in a manufacturing career that included part-time teaching as a business faculty at the local community college. I later moved to the department chair at that community college and then to director of extended campus services, then associate vice-president, and then president at the same college" (African-American Female).

Story 4: "I worked as an engineer with internal progression to more senior roles within the engineering company in another country. Later, I moved to the United States and began working at a manufacturing company in the automotive industry. While working in that position, I was invited to serve on a program advisory committee at a local community college. After serving on this committee, I was invited to apply for the Dean of Careers program at that community college and then transitioned to the Executive Director of Manufacturing programs and later to the Dean of Career and Technical Education at another City community college. Eventually, I became the Interim President at that college and later President in another community college but in that state" (Muslim Male).

Story 5: "I moved home and was recruited for the presidency by the prominent tribal member and faculty member at the local community college. The original design was to learn about the position over five years and then, when the president retired, to become president. However, within six months of being the Interim President, I became the President" (Native-American Female).

## ASCENDENCY PREPARATIONS

Each of the Sitting Presidents shared how they prepared explicitly for the ascendency of the presidency. While the Buttimer award recipients talked about the importance of working at the same college/district and participation in organized leadership development programs as central in the ascendancy preparation, the Sitting Presidents valued different ascendancy preparations, namely mentorship for obtaining specific skills.

## Mentorship

All but one sitting president mentioned that mentorship was the most critical ascendency preparation. A sitting president said that "mentors provided me great guidance and advice to adequately prepare for community college leadership" (Asian Male). Other sitting presidents shared that it is essential to have mentors from a wide selection of individuals. Many were leaders that they knew while still in the Dean position who showed them how to "be a good manager" (White Female), and who "helped [me] get the right support to get into leadership training institutes" (Asian Male). Other Sitting Presidents reflected that their mentor was an individual who was in the president position at their college and provided opportunities to:

> do large/complex projects and do college initiatives. My mentor particularly advised me to strengthen other areas in my leadership that needed to be developed and offered guidance on how to navigate and manage politics, media, contract negotiation, faculty, disgruntle personnel, personnel matters. (African-American Male)

At least one of the Sitting Presidents recalled that the president at another college became a mentor who "provided a Master Class on the presidency and allowed me to really see the role from the inside" (African-American Female).

The Sitting Presidents defined mentors as someone "who can speak on your behalf" (White Female). It is someone "that was intentional about helping me gain the experiences I would need to lead" (African-American Female). Finally, it was someone "which explored my career aspirations, personal strengths, and weaknesses, and gave me strategies to improve in areas of weaknesses" (Asian Male). One of the Sitting Presidents recalled that:

> before my presidency, I did not realize the power of mentorship . . . having someone who has experience, knowledge, and wisdom to guide me in my journey. . . someone who helped me in taking a broader perspective to resolve a problem. (Muslim Male)

There was a noted connection between race and ethnicity for mentoring. One sitting president said that:

> I was mentored informally by a wonderful Latina college president who believed I could be a successful college president. . . Because of her inspiration, I want to pay her efforts forward as I now serve as a mentor for the National Community College Hispanic Council. (Latinx Male)

Another sitting president said that:

> much of my mentoring came as informal relationships with phenomenal Indigenous leaders whom I either worked with or who were in my life by other means. I do not discount the relationships I have built through traditional/cultural means, as those are the ones I tend to fall back on when times are difficult. (Native-American Female)

## Obtain Specific Skills

The Buttimer Award recipients and the Sitting Presidents all agreed on the need to gain specific skills prior to becoming a president and agreed on what those skills entailed.

### Become an Expert

In becoming an expert, the Sitting Presidents focused on building their research skills and the specific skills of knowing how to use research to build a culture of evidence. One sitting president mentioned that it was essential to "know how to analyze data and lead the organization in developing a culture of data-informed decision-making" (White Female). Related was the importance of having a doctoral degree, which all the Sitting Presidents agreed was a prerequisite for the position. One sitting president shared that "not only do titles matter but having significant accomplishments in key areas as a result of those titles can carry more weight. The fit is extremely important" (African-American Female).

Aligned with becoming an expert is the need to build and master specific skills, such as "being good with grant administration, budgeting, staff supervision" (Native-American Male) or having "a decade-long experience in academic administration and community engagements"

(Muslim Male). Another sitting president shared their intentionality was to become an expert accordingly:

> When I was Vice President of Academic Affairs, there was a Vice President vacancy in Student Services, and I persuaded the President of the college to allow me to serve in both positions for eight months . . . that gave me additional high-level skills. (Latinx Female)

Finally, one sitting president summarized what the other Sitting Presidents expressed about the need to acquire specific and important skills, in that the most important of all skills is "simply one skill: People skills, People skills, and People skills" (Muslim Male).

### Problem Solving

The Sitting Presidents defined problem-solving as a skill as well as a strategy. As a skill, problem-solving was based on "having a fine mind, being resolve, being action-orientated" (White Male). As a strategy, problem-solving allowed one to be "willing to face each challenge head-on with a strategy to overcome the challenges. You must also be an actor and be able to navigate all situations without showing your hand" (African-American Male). Finally, problem-solving was seen as an inherent part of being an entrepreneur in terms of "being creative and finding and securing revenues (stable and predictable sources of revenue will become outdated) to fund people, programs, technology, and deteriorating facilities" (Asian Male).

### Networking

Unlike the Buttimer award recipients who used networking strategically to make personal connections that would open doors, the Sitting Presidents used networking to gain more skills that would be useful in their upward pathways. One president mentioned the need to "purposefully gain experience by looking for opportunities to get involved in the academic side of the college" (White Male).

### Introspection

Similar to the Buttimer award recipients, the Sitting Presidents shared that introspection was the beginning point for success. A common refrain in the interviews of the Sitting Presidents was to "be yourself." One president shared, "I started with knowing thyself by asking: Do I have what it takes to serve as a college president" (Asian Male). Another added, "It began for me by being true to myself and reflecting on my internal compass that is based on my values and beliefs. I was called on to serve and to become a change agent" (Asian Female). Finally, another shared:

> one lesson I learned is just to be yourself and try not to project to be someone that you are not. What has worked for me is to be as authentic as possible as people around you appreciate that as a quality in the presidency. (Latinx Male)

## REFLECTIONS ON WHAT IT TAKES TO BE SUCCESSFUL

Like the Buttimer award recipients, the Sitting Presidents shared the same categories for what it took for them to be successful in the presidential position.

### Context

The context for the Buttimer award recipients was being aware of post-secondary education trends and knowledge of how other presidents at various institutions were responding to those trends. For the Sitting Presidents, context meant something different. It meant learning about the college as a singular institution with the intent to have a better interview for the president position. Some also related the context to learning about the community college as something that would allow them to work as a president more efficiently. Central in this process is to "learn as much about the college prior to which you are applying" (Latinx Female), with attention on learning the "character and history of the college" (White Female) and "the participatory governance, respective roles of faculty, and the Board" (White Male). One president "made a few trips (before starting the position officially) to meet with the district chancellor, trustees, and college leaders to collect information on where the college is on budgeting, accreditation, strategic plan, and urgent matters," and yet cautioned that:

> it is not realistic for a new president coming from the outside to learn everything about the college before accepting a job offer. Doing thorough research on the college and contacting one's professional network around the country can help, but it is never enough. I wish I knew more about the significant nuances of institutional culture before I started my previous and current positions. I wish I did more research about the community, including the cost of living, political environment, pressing issues, to name a few. (African-American Male)

## Vision

Like the Buttimer awardees, the Sitting Presidents talked about the necessity to formulate a vision and then live by that vision to create and sustain educational changes for the community college. The "servant leader" term was used repeatedly by the Sitting Presidents; as one said, "in addition to specific leadership competencies, the position often demands to let go of personal ego, stamina, humility, creativity, and resilience. It is the role of a servant leader" (Asian Male). Other components in building the vision were to be "resilient and persistent all at the same time" (White Female).

## Motivations

The Sitting Presidents reflected on their motivations in several ways, but the central theme was the joy of changing lives for the better. One president shared, "it is a privilege and an honor to serve my tribe and our students in this capacity, and I do not take a moment of it for granted" (Native-American Female). Another said that "I am motivated to fight to make it possible for all to have access and achieve our American dreams" (Asian Female). Yet another president said:

> I am privileged to know that my role has had an impact on changing the lives and destinies of students. As the only member of my family to graduate from high school and college, I personally know the benefits of higher education and try to promote that to those I serve. (White Male)

The concept of opportunity was another critical motivator that was often linked by the Sitting Presidents as essential to being a change agent. One sitting president shared:

> the opportunity to make a difference and to serve as a Change Agent . . . to see the change in someone's life. My best reward is when I hear from a student directly telling me how his/her educational experience at the college has changed his/her and sometimes the entire family's lives. Words cannot express the sense of fulfillment. (African-American Female)

Similarly, another president said:

> what motivates me is knowing that I have a special opportunity to provide leadership in a community that I feel understands a

community that I understand. I consider it a privilege to be able to improve the lives of people from all levels of society and for low income and ethnic minority students. I am determined to increase access (enrollment) and student success outcomes for all students. (Latinx Male)

Figure 12.1 Word mapping: Sitting Presidents motivations.

The word mapping shown in Figure 12.1 for the Sitting Presidents shows a different pattern than the word mapping for the Buttimer awardees. The Buttimer awardees mostly mentioned being creative, caring, having patience, focusing, and having passion. The most mentioned words for the Sitting Presidents were changing lives, duty, being a change-agent, and like the Buttimer awardees to have passion.

## CHALLENGES AND STRATEGIES USED TO OVERCOME CHALLENGES WHILE IN THE JOB

Both the Buttimer awardees and the Sitting Presidents reflected on similar challenges that they experienced in their first year on the job. The Sitting Presidents also identified the process of on-boarding as a primary challenge.

## On-Boarding

The Sitting Presidents shared three strategies that they used during their boarding preparation.

### Intentionality

Intentionality included researching the college and meeting with key college stakeholders. One president shared that research included:

> getting information from the college about the college. It should include the latest accreditation report, strategic plan, financial audit reports, and president's direct reports and reading them before arriving at work. I also got the names of faculty, staff, student leaders, and community leaders whom I must meet, and I met all the recommended people within the first two months. (African-American Male)

Another president reflected on intentionally making choices to arrange:

> meetings with each vice president and then with faculty leaders and deans, as well as the various constituent groups. I asked each group or individual to suggest three people in the community I needed to meet. Then, I proceeded to meet with the community members. (Latinx Female)

## Networking

A second strategy to overcome challenges while on the job involved networking in initiating relationships and enhancing existing relationships. One president shared:

> I used existing networks to have a clear understanding of the system's priorities. I was fortunate that an interim president was in place, and she began to communicate with me the day that I was named. I began to get involved with things such as the budgeting process prior to my official start date. (African-American Female)

Likewise, another sitting president identified the importance of reaching out to other presidents in the same state, noting:

> I am grateful for the presence of other presidents in the state who were more than willing to assist and mentor me in any way they

> could. I think I have learned the most from my fellow tribal college presidents over any training I could have participated in. (Native-American Female)

### Stakeholder Collaboration

Finally, another president shared the importance of identifying and then reaching out to key players in the community:

> I reached out and asked them to educate me by providing some historical background on critical issues related to the community. I believe it is important to know the weather forecast in the community and the people whom you can trust and who want you to succeed. They can help you identify challenging issues and concerns before they become unwieldy. On-boarding done properly is crucial. (Asian Female)

## Purposeful Decisions Made During the First Week of Employment

Another strategy mentioned by the Sitting Presidents to overcome challenges was to be realistic about one's vision and the likelihood to use that vision in the new position. One of the Sitting Presidents reflected on the importance of planning to make purposeful decisions even during the first week of employment to advance that vision as a way to "hit the ground running" (Native-American Female).

One sitting president strategically:

> did a comprehensive visit to all colleges in the system . . . followed by a couple of community meet and greet events . . . that provided me with an excellent opportunity to have a face-to-face conversation with community leaders and stakeholders and to share my background and experiences. As a follow-up to these events, I sent a personal note of thanks to community leaders and stakeholders. (Muslim Male)

## Time

Another strategy mentioned by many of the Sitting Presidents, and that was similar to the Buttimer awardees, was the desire to have had more time to prepare, more time to do their research on their new institution, and more time to do networking before their start date. One president said,

"I wish I had more time prior to my start date to simply look at data, ask questions and learn more about the college" (African-American Female). Another sitting president said that more time would have enabled "an opportunity to spend some structured time with executive leadership and to learn about their priorities and shared vision of the College, including the top-down hierarchical structure that was new to me" (Muslim Male).

## Personal-Level Challenges

The Sitting Presidents shared personal challenges that they felt they needed to overcome for overall success. Many alluded that a primary challenge was simply realizing that they were doing something new and that new is always challenging. One of the Sitting President's said, "change is challenging and scary, but it also is a good thing" (Native-American Female). Another president said that strategies were useful in overcoming stress as "there is never enough time, but planning helps overcome this" (White Male). However, another president shared the need to learn from and with mistakes: "What I dislike is making mistakes at this level. You are ultimately responsible for your own decisions, but often you are responsible for others at the institution. Unlike other administrative positions that I have held, I have less "cover" for the mistakes that I make, so be very deliberate and consultative when making decisions" (Latinx Male).

Finally, a president shared that "I have worked on being a good listener, being extremely patient, being inclusive in decision-making. I want to emphasize how important it is to be honest with yourself, to have humility, and to have a positive outlook on life" (Latinx Male).

## Institutional-Level Challenges

Institutional-level challenges depended on the particular community college as each responded to unique student communities and unique internal politics. Nevertheless, the Sitting Presidents mentioned five similar challenges that created particular difficulties during their first year in service. The first challenge included "understanding the context of the board and community relations and key stakeholders such as unions and faculty senate" (Muslim Male). The second challenge was the need to do more and better research on the community at large, because:

> more knowledge and understanding in my region before I arrived here, including a stronger introduction and some time to study the community, would have been preferred. Presidents are perceived

> to be the face and voice of the colleges they lead. Not knowing your communities well can lead to problems, even disasters. (Asian Female)

The third challenge included the need to build positive relationships within the complexity of the new position. It included finding out "whom to talk to first and whom to trust" (African-American Male). The fourth challenge included understanding existing problems at the college and the contexts of those programs, which as one sitting president shared, included a need to have "a review by the Board of Trustees indicating some of the messes that would be uncovered" (White Male). The final challenge included building honest relationships. One sitting president said that "trying to develop internal and external relationships while still learning is challenging. I feel as if I am building an airplane while it is already in the air - my job is to keep it aloft" (African-American Female).

Additionally, the Sitting Presidents mentioned their preference for better skills to help identify and work toward addressing the institutional challenges. It included "managing politics (internal and external)" (African-American Male), "working with a micro-managing Board" (White Male), having more knowledge on "facilities construction and management" (Latinx Female), on "fund-raising strategies" (White Male), on "running large budgets" (Native-American Female) and on "working with the media/public relations" (African-American Male).

## SHARED STRATEGIES FOR FUTURE SUCCESS

The Sitting Presidents shared what specific strategies they felt they needed for success in the presidency position.

### Knowledge of Federal Policies and Reforms

Knowledge of federal policies was deemed necessary by all the Sitting Presidents. For some, federal policies coincided with their vision, such as "legislative call for drastic increases in graduation and completion rates, and for addressing the mismatch between the demand for skilled workers and supply for a qualified and trained workforce" (Asian Male). For others, knowing national and state policies was the foundation for communicating these policies with college stakeholders and leading the college to change. One president shared that "I needed to share how national and state policies overlap as with the new funding formulas that guide all choices within the institution" (White Female).

Another president shared the importance of understanding state policies and mandates and to be able to communicate to faculty and staff:

> to ensure that all constituents understand the funding formula and the metrics, such as AB705, that the college now much use to determine the allocation model and to share this information with faculty and staff to identify strategies and activities designed to meet the mandates. (Latinx Female)

While some Sitting Presidents used federal policies to anchor advocacy "to reach out to others to demonstrate the value of a community college education to our local, state, and national leaders" (Asian Female), other presidents felt the constraints of federal policies as "they have negative implications on so much of the work we try and do at community colleges" (White Male).

## Budget Issues

Economic impacts were linked to shrinking federal, state, and local budgets. Sitting Presidents in this area shared three themes. First was how to run the college with declining state and local revenue. One president shared:

> our extreme dependence on state and local revenue as well as tuition continues to put us at the mercy of the "ups and downs" of the state economy. We need to hire community college leaders who are experienced at building political capital with key policy leaders in the political and business sectors. (Latinx Female)

The second budget issue was the need to be entrepreneurial in terms of envisioning alternative practices. One president shared that "we need to continue to find ways to mitigate the cost of books and materials, and we need to support alternative ways in which we provide instruction for credit" (Latinx Male). Finally, the third budget issue was a focus on serving low-income, nontraditional students and their communities. Many of the Sitting Presidents talked about the importance of ensuring that "people who are low income, first-generation, and ethnic minority continue to have access to community colleges. The cost of attending community colleges needs to be restrained" (White Female).

Another identified the common theme related to budget issues focuses on the repercussions of current economic times, which made "difficult financial situations force students into homelessness, and systemic disrespect for those in poverty and the lack of assistance for those who need an additional boost to enjoy the benefits of higher education is needed" (White Male). Another president shared that "we have a low unemployment rate yet high areas of poverty all around which complicates access" (African-American Female).

Finally, all Sitting Presidents shared the need to connect economic impact to a vision that, in turn, would be used to guide future reform efforts. As shared by one sitting president:

> I am of the opinion that the college is here to serve the community and should do everything within reason to meet its needs, including offering job training programs, developing business opportunities, community investment programs, and especially programs to carry on the tribal language. As a rural location with little manufacturing employment, creating more opportunities is a high priority for me. (Native-American Male)

## Collective Bargaining

While the Buttimer recipients all talked about complications in the collective bargaining process, this was less of an issue for the Sitting Presidents. The Sitting Presidents all talked positively about building and using collective teams for forwarding change. Nevertheless, one president commented on the personality issues that can arise within the process of collective bargaining in which "an environment exists that permits people to behave badly. Just the notion of spreading misinformation as a strategy is taking its toll on civility within the college setting" (White Female).

## Management

Both the Buttimer recipients and the Sitting Presidents placed tremendous importance on presidential and board relations. The Sitting Presidents mentioned the need to understand "the political leanings of the board and what drives them" (White Male) and to have a solid understanding of "accreditation standards as a way to provide a good picture of how an institution should operate" (White Female). Many of the Sitting

Presidents also mentioned that the lack of African-American, Latino, Native-American, and Asian faculty and senior administrators is critical. As one president shared:

> While our country is gradually becoming more diverse racially and ethnically, the underrepresentation of people of color in the classroom continues to be a chronic problem. Success rates for students of color need to improve dramatically. Community college leaders need to demonstrate not by words but through impactful strategic actions that they value equitable student success and the hiring of a more ethnically diverse administration, faculty, and staff. (Latinx Male)

Another noted the value of a liberal arts education in today's economic climate, social justice, and access (Native-American Female).

## Student Learning Outcomes

Teaching and learning issues and trends related to increasing student learning outcomes were seen as necessary by all of the Sitting Presidents. Student learning was connected to building human capital that "as a result of the large retirement boom, had increasing importance in narrowing the performance gap between high- and low-performing student populations, addressing issues of income inequities, homelessness, and the disconnected youths" (Asian Male). Similarly, as one president said, "the ability to lead and focus the institutional resources, personnel and financial, to graduate and complete a much greater percentage of students, in a shorter period, with much fewer resources is exhilarating" (Asian Male). Specific skill's training was linked to student success.

One president said that the focus should be on introducing college-ready skills for those "under-prepared students to address their lack of college readiness" (African-American Male). Another president said:

> our challenge is to keep students who choose to stop out and work while attracting low-income students to attend. We have skills gaps in some critical areas. However, low enrollment in that same program (ex. IT) is of major concern. (African-American Female)

New pedagogy was linked to skills training with "informational technology tools bringing great promise for revolutionizing the process of teaching and learning" (Asian Male).

Finally, the ability to organize and offer academic programs that are responsive and relevant to the ever-changing workforce needs amid the complex political environment of the local community were seen as essential to promote student learning. For example:

> although some colleges are offering such services, student insecurities impact overall learning. Finally, one president noted, in particular, concern about working with the local food bank to stock a food pantry on campus and help provide referrals to local social service agencies. (Latinx Female)

## Social Reforms

Each of the Sitting Presidents elaborated on the social reforms needed and used to help their students and their communities. First-generation students' issues, marginalization, systemic racism, and a lack of senior administrator diversity were targeted as among the most critical areas for social reform. One president concluded that:

> there is a need to continue focusing on the marginalization and systemic forms of exclusion affecting people of color and other underrepresented groups. The dearth of Latino college presidents continues to be an ongoing problem that demonstrates how decision-makers do not value the multiple assets that we bring to the table. Those assets include possessing an intimate knowledge of Latino culture and language that can be most helpful when interacting with Latino and other diverse communities. (Latinx Male)

Another president reflected on the needs of students, saying:

> We are catering to the academic and non-academic needs of many first-generation, historically underserved populations. For most of them, community college is the only option to pursue their higher education journey as they cannot afford the rising costs of attending a four-year university. (Muslim Male)

Eventually, the vision of helping others is part of the reason for social reforms, as shared by another president:

> Politically, social injustices are destroying the lives of millions, especially the poor and underserved populations of our country. It prevents people from achieving their highest aspirations and reduces our workforce pool. Consistently it is reducing our ability to compete nationally and internationally. (African-American Female)

## Personal Strategies for Success

Like the Buttimer awardees, the Sitting Presidents also listed strategies to overcome the most difficult challenges. Unlike the Buttimer recipients, the Sitting Presidents focused more on coping and personal health and intersectionality complications.

### Self-Reflection

Self-reflection was a personality component that many of the Sitting Presidents found to be essential. Self-reflection begins by considering what it means to be ready. One president shared that "I wish someone told me much earlier that you do not have to be ready to apply for a college presidency because no one is ever totally ready" (Asian Male). Another shared that:

> I wish I had known that I would be presented with the leadership opportunity well before I would feel I was ready. However, if we wait until we are ready, we will wait forever. Sometimes it is not a question of readiness. It is a question of "Are you willing?". (Native-American Female)

Similarly, another president shared that "I do not think one is ever fully prepared to become a community college president. However, if you are willing to make mistakes, be honest about them, and make earnest efforts to improve, that should be good preparation" (Asian Female). Yet another president shared that it is important to "not take challenges and criticism personally and always maintain strong ethical standards" (African-American Male). Another president explained that:

> Everyone needs to recognize that there are many ways to get to the presidency, but you must first answer the question, Why do you

> want to be a president, and if it is not for the right reasons, then do not pursue the job. (Asian Female)

Finally, a president shared that it is critical to "be confident in your skills and abilities and highlight these while working on those that need to be improved and most of all to believe in yourself and be persistent" (Latinx Male).

### Time Management

The Sitting Presidents identified time management as a critical strategy for success. They shared the importance of having a critical lens on time management to keep control of the calendar. One president said that "every day is a new day in the life of a college president" (Muslim Male). Another mentioned that "when you hit the ground running, and you want an open-door environment and yet find yourself trying to accommodate everyone. It does not give you time to prepare or plan" (African-American Female). Nevertheless, another president shared that:

> the complexity and demands that are what I like most. On any given day, I will have several meetings with a wide variety of constituent groups, ranging from local business owners, community-based advocates for disadvantaged groups, division deans, student leaders, and members of our executive cabinet. There is not enough time to participate in meetings and synthesize all the information that needs to be gathered and evaluated. Count on responding to emails long after 5:00 p.m. and make sure you respond to emails as soon as possible. (African-American Female)

Eventually, a sitting president shared that "nobody likes it when a college president is perceived to be unresponsive" (Latinx Male).

### Coping and Personal Health

An important area of advice given by all the Sitting Presidents was concerning making personal choices that favor balance in one's personal life. One president shared that "presidents need to be ready to work extremely hard and to make personal sacrifices, but one must have a life outside the job. Keeping a healthy balance is paramount" (African-American Male). Similarly, another said, "I wish someone had told me to remember that you are always 'on.' If you want to have fun, go out of town!" (Latinx Female). The same president shared that "I walk on campus daily and, generally, have one glass of wine in the evening. I try to talk to faculty and staff at all levels" (Latinx Female).

The Sitting Presidents shared three ways to cope with the stressors involved in being a president. The first is to maintain balance, as:

> balance helps make wise decisions rooted in my values. When they are vetted with our leadership team's key members, it helps them know who you are. It also reminds me that to remain in my position; I am dependent on their assessment and perceptions of my performance, and, ultimately, me. (Latinx Male)

The idea of balance was also linked to the ability to:

> compartmentalize some issues, listen, reflect, and speak with a trusted colleague or two. I also talk with my spouse (a retired psychologist) and not let most of the negative talk matter. I also exercise and remain positive and confident in my abilities. (White Male)

Conclusively, the complexities of balance were noted to be embedded in the position, as one president shared that "I struggle with the expectation that a college president can solve all problems, including making magic" (Asian Male).

The second area of advice was to know your capabilities. As one president shared:

> believing in my leadership abilities and approach each day with a positive perspective, a new beginning, I remain focused on students (African-American Male). Similarly, another advised the need for "upcoming administrators to understand they need to separate themselves as individuals from being the president." On the one hand, they cannot take things personally. On the other, the authority of the president rests in the position, not in the individual. "Keep the two separate and do not take yourself too seriously". (White Female)

Another president shared that:

> there will be plenty of challenges every day for a college president. It helps to remind ourselves of our job's great purpose: making a positive difference for the students and community we serve. The sense of being mission-driven helps put into perspective difficult issues at hand. (African-American Female)

The third strategy shared by the Sitting Presidents focused on maintaining physical and mental health, which all acknowledged as important even within a complicated and overly busy schedule. One president reflected that:

> self-care is critically important. I eat well, I exercise, and I take mental breaks during the day. I am available for what is crucially important in my life: my family. I do not ever want to be in a position where I must choose between my children or my job, and thankfully, my Board is quite supportive of that. I love the changeability of the work and the feeling that I am truly making a difference for my people. (Native-American Female)

Another president shared:

> Let me be honest and straightforward. When you arrive at the presidency, your normal life is over. This includes your spouse and children. Luckily, my children are all grown, and my husband supports me in every way. Humorously, he calls himself the unpaid chief of staff at home. He and I are partners, and I am very thankful. The presidency is a very lonely job yet extremely demanding, especially in this age of digital connectivity. You are concerned about and connected to the college 24–7. Students, parents, staff, and community members expect to hear from you when they want to. You are never disconnected. (Asian Female)

## Intersectionality and prejudice

Many of the presidents mentioned the need to understand the unique circumstances of being presidents of color and presidents who are LGBTQ. A Sitting President shared that as "community colleges are diverse, presidents who lead these colleges ought to be diverse" (Asian Female). Many of the Sitting Presidents shared that they were treated differently because of their race and ethnic heritages and gender. One Sitting President shared the need to "get accustomed to being viewed differently by everyone than ever before" (Muslim Male). Another said that "as a Chinese immigrant who speaks with an accent, I had additional challenges to convince people that Asian stereotypes do not fairly describe my abilities and capacities" (Asian Male). One president shared the need "to push oneself because I realized that I had as much (and in some cases more) to offer as the male administrators" (Latinx Female).

Another president warned of the need to:

> prepare to go through the *imposter syndrome*, especially as a person of color, as a woman, being from the LGBTQ, disabled, or other communities that are under-represented in community college presidencies. There will be times when you will wonder whether you are a "fit" for this role. (Latinx Male)

Similarly, a president shared that "as a man who is gay, I spent most of my life exceeding everyone's expectations since I was always nervous about being fired for being gay, which is still permissible in the Commonwealth of Pennsylvania" (White Male). Finally, one president shared what could have been beneficial in dealing with prejudice: "I wish I knew a gay or lesbian president in 2003 since my husband and I were the targets of hate crimes shortly after arriving at my second presidency" (White Male). Many of the Sitting Presidents reflected on issues of intersectionality and prejudice. It was without being prompted to do so, which is critical as it uncovers what some presidents encounter in the role of president, but it demonstrates issues of crucial concern.

## Summary of Advice

The narratives from the Sitting Presidents are essential to place a leadership context in the 2010s and the 2020s, and the future. Three Sitting Presidents gave three critical pieces of advice for future presidential candidates to consider. One Sitting President shared that it is necessary to "be strong, confident and ethical" (African-American Male). Another president shared that it is necessary to have a "purpose of being clear on wanting to make a difference and to have humility because the president is not all-powerful or invincible" (White Female). Lastly, another president shared the importance of "being an anchor in the community that supports your vision and to use leadership to be an effective change agent. Equally is to be an anchor in your home (spouse, significant other), which is extremely important to stabilizing the president's work" (Asian Female).

## REFERENCES

Garza Mitchell, R. L., & Cano-Monreal, G. L. (2015). Strategic planning for new presidents: Developing an entrance plan. *Community College Journal of Research and Practice*, 39(2), 113–121.

Garza Mitchell, R. L., & Eddy, P. L. (2008). In the middle: Career pathway of midlevel community college leaders. *Community College Journal of Research and Practice*, 32(10), 793–811. doi:10.1080/10668920802325739.

Raby, R. L., & Valeau, E. J. (2019). Position training and succession planning for community college international education leaders. *Community College Journal of Research and Practice*. On-LineFirst. Published July 26. doi:10.1080/10668926.2019.1645055.

Wiseman, I. M., & Vaughan, G. B. (1988). *The community college presidency*. American Association of Community Colleges.

Chapter Thirteen

# Comparative Profiles – Buttimer Awardees and Sitting College Presidents

## COMPARATIVE PROFILES

The previous chapters profiled two groups of community college presidents to learn about their leadership pathways and understand their narratives, what they considered necessary to prepare for and be a leader during their presidency. This chapter compares the Buttimer awardees and the Sitting Presidents to identify commonly shared experiences, leadership styles, and expectations. It must be noted that there are two significant differences between these groups of leaders that influence their narratives. First, Buttimer awardees are only from California. Many of the awardees were presidents in three different decades, the late 1990s, 2000s, and 2010s. Second, Sitting Presidents come from throughout the country. They are current in their position and reflect leadership experiences during the mid-to-late 2010s. Table 13.1 shows a leadership comparison of the Buttimer presidents and the Sitting Presidents.

## LEADERSHIP PREPARATION

Comparison information shows how Buttimer awardees and Sitting Presidents narrate their pathway experiences and define what they see as essential characteristics for presidential leaders. Comparisons are shared across three broad categories: motivations, skill sets, and problem-solving strategies.

**Table 13.1 Comparing Perspectives of Buttimer and Sitting Presidents**

| Category | Buttimer | Sitting |
|---|---|---|
| Motivations | Creative; caring; be focused; have a passion | Duty; privilege to serve; change lives for the better; have passion |
| Vision | Defined by passions; be well articulated; be fluid to change with context | Defined by "servant-leader"; be well articulated; use to make purposeful decisions |
| Personality | Be honest; be ethical | Be persistent; be confident; be ethical; have humility |
| **Building a Skill Set** | | |
| Intentionality | Embark on a traditional career pathway; get teaching assignments | Do long-term planning to research opportunities; strategically change one job for another |
| Work in the same district | Critical importance | Not important |
| Enroll in a leadership preparation program | Critical importance; assess skills and get new ones | Critical importance; assess skills and get new ones |
| Mentorship | Keep old mentors and build new ones | Purposefully find mentors at Dean and President levels; race/ethnicity enhances mentorship |
| Networking | Critically important; need to build networking skills | Part of intentionality to initiate and enhance existing networks |
| Become an expert | Part of lifelong learning; helps to advance vision<br>Part of introspection in terms of what skills are needed | Linked to professional development to gain skills, especially research<br>Get a doctorate and publish Master-specific skills, such as budgeting and political advocacy |
| **Problem-Solving Strategies** | | |
| Know the context | Know sociopolitical and economic issues of higher education; learn how other CEOs are responding to similar contexts; learn about how these issues affect the college | Know sociopolitical and economic issues of that college, including research about the college and talking to stakeholders; know how federal policies and how poverty impacts the college; know budget constraints and how to be entrepreneurial |
| Problem-solving skills | Identify the problem; Invite others into the problem-solving process; use research to ground your vision and inform decision-making; take risks only when necessary | Know what skills need to be developed and build a strategy to overcome challenges; be entrepreneurial to think creatively |

| Category | Buttimer | Sitting |
|---|---|---|
| Leadership strategies | Build respect; fairly address difficult situations; be professional and do not change to please others; be self-confident; recognize other's expertise and empower them | Be self-confident; Know how to work with different personalities; be an anchor in the community |
| Communication | Be a good listener; Share; be consistent and communicate often | Communicate frequently and in a timely manner; Be a good listener |
| Time | Use time wisely; prepare wisely | Need more time to prepare |
| Personal level | Build and keep respect; build effective teams | Honor learning and realize it is OK to make mistakes; be honest with yourself and have humility |
| Institutional level | Build teams to embrace your vision; focus on budget issues; conduct community outreach | Research college and community; understand the complexity of stakeholders; Build honesty in these relationships |
| Collective bargaining | Know the pitfalls of collective bargaining; work with micromanaging boards; practice effective team building | Work with collective bargaining; Work with micromanaging boards; work to increase the diversity of faculty and senior administrators |
| Student learning outcomes | Critical importance | Critical importance; focus on new pedagogies, like IT |
| Social reforms | Not much of an issue | Focus on the marginalization of students and systemic forms of exclusion; build equity for nontraditional students; focus on homelessness and food insecurity that complicates learning |
| **Strategies for Success** | | |
| Self-reflection | Not mentioned | What it means to be ready; why want to be president |
| Time management | Critically important | Deal with complexities to serve all |
| Coping and personal health | Be healthy, body and mind | A healthy balance of work/self-time; ground choices why you want to serve; make self-care part of every day |
| Intersectionality | Biases from former colleagues, as you got promoted; biases about age | Circumstances of being presidents of color, LGBTQ, Female; dealing with prejudice |

## Motivations

Each of the presidents interviewed for this book had their reason for wanting to be a community college president. Despite their different backgrounds, their motivations, vision for change, and their importance on vision were similar. Regarding motivations, the Buttimer recipients talked more about their role as a president. It aligned with the traditional literature regarding the need to be creative, caring, and focused. It differed from the Sitting Presidents whose reflection on why they wanted to be a president aligned more with the current literature in linking their motivation to being a servant-leader and seeing their leadership as a duty in changing lives. Both groups of presidents highlighted the importance of wanting to work with others to influence change positively; as one Sitting President said, "what is clear is that the presidency is not a career option for people who want to work by themselves" (Native-American Female). Ultimately, both the Buttimer recipients and the Sitting Presidents placed passion as their primary motivation.

## Presidential Skill Sets

Both the Buttimer recipients and the Sitting Presidents shared very similar ideas of the essential skill sets that presidents need to possess. These skill sets coincide directly with the American Association of Community Colleges list of competencies for leadership. There was also a noted similarity in how all the presidents defined how they gained these skills. Intentionality was a central process in which all the presidents built their skill sets. It included enrollment in leadership preparation programs, building mentorship and networking skills, and becoming an expert. While both groups of presidents honored expertise, there was no consensus on what an expert meant. For the Buttimer recipients, expertise was seen as part of a lifelong learning strategy that would advance their vision. For the Sitting Presidents, expertise was intentionally linked to gaining research skills, budget and finance skills, and political advocacy skills.

A primary difference between the Buttimer recipients and the Sitting Presidents was that the Buttimer had defined skill-building as a passive endeavor while the Sitting Presidents viewed it as a requirement grounded in intentionality. For example, the Buttimer recipients embarked on traditional career pathways with prescriptive jobs up the career ladder. The pathway was not one that stemmed from choice. It represented the only option that they had for promotion. Their career pathway aligned with most of them already working in the same district and in the same college where they eventually became president. The Sitting Presidents had varied career pathways and placed importance on strategic planning on how to change one job for the other, even choices that were not part of a traditional pathway. However, once in the community college system, these presidents continued to make strategic and intentional choices, including changing institutions, changing cities, and changing states. A final difference was the emphasis placed on race/ethnicity and gender in the mentorship and networking context by the Sitting Presidents, who felt that their intersectionality determined their presidential experiences.

## Problem-Solving Strategies

The Buttimer recipients and Sitting Presidents shared similar responses to defining problem-solving strategies. Two categories of problem-solving strategies were identified: personal skills needed to solve problems and institutional problems that needed to be solved.

### Personal Skills

In terms of personal skills that would help solve problems, all presidents considered their ability to communicate, be a good listener, and identify and build collaborative teams as part of their most critical personal skill sets – likewise, each identified time as a critical element to prepare for their new role as president. The two groups of presidents also shared similar personal characteristics that they felt were needed to be an effective leader, including addressing difficult situations, working with different personalities, and being self-confident.

The problem-solving techniques of the two groups of presidents, however, differed slightly. The Buttimer recipients used a prescriptive problem-solving process in which they identified the problem, used research to inform decision-making, grounded their choices in their vision, and then used collaboration to problem-solve. Their focus was on building teams and keeping the respect of those teams. While also prescriptive, the Sitting Presidents were more inclined to stress creativity and applied entrepreneurial thinking to formulate action items. In this respect, they focused on honoring learning new things, realizing that it is permissible to make mistakes, and humility to ground future decisions.

### Skills to Solve Institutional Problems

Both Buttimer and Sitting Presidents identified similar institutional problems that they felt needed to be addressed using specific problem-solving strategies. Both groups of presidents identified challenges in budget management, in the collective bargaining process, in working with micromanaging boards, meeting student success initiatives, and in the varied sociopolitical and economic problems that impacted the institution.

However, each group of presidents also shared distinctive differences in how they identified these problems and what specific problem-solving strategies they adopted. While the Buttimer awardees looked more to create institutional change, the Sitting Presidents focused more on learning why the issues existed and then creatively imagining how to define a change process unique to each problem. The Buttimer awardees were also interested in how other CEOs responded to similar problems, and then strategically used the knowledge to align their vision and focus on what changes they would adopt. The Sitting Presidents instead focused on getting research on the college and on research from the field to then apply that research on how federal policies and state policies impacted their college. In this way, the Sitting Presidents were most interested in how poverty negatively affected student learning. Finally, while the Buttimer awardees ignored the intersection of race and gender as an institutional problem, the Sitting Presidents focused on systemic forms of exclusion based on race, gender, and LGBTQI+ status and marginalization of non-traditional students.

## Challenges of Management and Leadership

Both the Buttimer and Sitting Presidents shared similar stories about the challenges of management and leadership. All mentioned the need to be aware of "a steep learning curve in which the workload increased exponentially". Likewise, both shared the importance of using critical thinking to prioritize work but as well to build the necessary skills to "not say 'yes' to everything."

## Personal Considerations

All the presidents placed importance on personal well-being in terms of having a healthy body and mind. They were interconnected in identifying and then using efficient time-management strategies to deal with daily problems, manage communication effectively, and deal with institutional complexities while maintaining one's health. As one Buttimer awardee shared, "there is a need to put appropriate boundaries in place as to when to stop work." There were also differences in how each group of presidents perceived health. The Sitting Presidents consistently talked about self-reflection regarding what it means to be a president and what it means to be ready as part of a strategic decision-making construct. It was not an issue talked about by any of the Buttimer awardees. Finally, both presidents talked about biases against them and how they helped build their professional identities. The Buttimer recipients talked about biases that they received from former colleagues when they moved up the ranks and their colleagues did not, and some mentioned the biases they received due to their age. However, the Sitting Presidents did not mention these biases, but instead talked about intersectionality and the prejudices they received by being presidents of color, women, and members of the LGBTQI+ community.

## Summary

The differences between the Buttimer Presidents and the Sitting Presidents are grounded in the times in which they lead. The Buttimer Presidents clearly reflected the interests of the 1990s that reflects the entry of the Millennials to community college leadership. Those who led in the 1990s showed continuity in leadership styles with the previous generation of leaders. Those who led in the 2000s showed affinity to those new leadership best practices that reflected specific past changes. Likewise, the Sitting Presidents represent the oldest Millennials who were greatly influenced by this century's events, which grounded a new leadership style unique to their generation. As such, many of the preferred competencies question the past leadership styles that keep the status quo a viable alternative for aspiring community college CEOs of the future.

Chapter Fourteen

# The Story of Clementine

No presidency is attainable without the required experience, which accumulates challenging work and, yes, some luck. Nevertheless, as shown in this book, many other contexts exist that help defines who you are as a leader and what steps are needed to be ready for the presidency, especially the first position (Jones & Warnick, 2012). In this cauldron of ascendancy, preparation is multidimensional and complex. The takeaway from this story is a realization that no job should be too small or menial, from sweeping the floor, working in the dining area, helping prepare the stage, co-teaching a class, shadowing a counselor, or learning something about the jobs and the people who populate them. It is the best use of one's time and talent on the way up.

## THE STORY OF CLEMENTINE

One Buttimer awardee's journey provides an example. The name is fictional to protect the individual's identity. Clementine began her career as a store clerk, where she first developed the knack for meeting people, communicating well, and being friendly and helpful. Unknown to her at the time, these skills would serve her well in later years. Upon graduating from a lesser-known college, she landed her first part-time teaching job in a small junior high school. In the department, she was chosen as the spokesperson because no one else wanted the job. Because of her then style, she met with success, and people gravitated toward her.

She later moved to another state where she got a full-time job at a junior high school. There, she coached girls' volleyball and taught math. As a result of winning success, she was asked to be the vice principal in charge of girls. Concurrently, she taught math at a local community college. When the job for the full-time vice principal was announced, she applied but was not chosen. Soon after that, Clementine moved to a new high school district office, where she became a coordinator responsible for curriculum integration. Her part-time job at the community college also changed as she began to work in curriculum integration. All the while, she showed her prowess with writing and speaking, and soon became an accepted member by the schools as someone associated with the district office that could be trusted. Her work led to interactions with the County Office of Schools, where she worked with curriculum leaders and other administrative heads across the county. She was learning the art of collaborating with teachers and earning their respect and the campus and district administration.

Clementine spent several years in this position, until she considered applying for an assistant dean of instruction job at a local community college. The job emphasis was on curriculum development and faculty support. At the time, she explains, "the job description was not very clear, and more disturbing, it was federally funded and would not be renewed if funding was not secured for the following year." Also complicating her decision was that she was married with three young children, and she already had job security and tenure.

However, Clementine decided to apply and was successful. She was assigned to various college committees by her Dean of Instruction, where she often became the notetaker, as clerical help was not provided to the committees. Her role on committees grew. Moreover, she acquired new skills (listening and recalling details and facts) related to college management and personnel. She successfully rewrote the grant, which gave her another year to breathe and live in the system. Throughout the district, she was placed on committees involving budget planning and development and human relations, which took her beyond the college walls and deep into new territories. She was never afraid to take on new challenges and learn new things; she offered her support, where it was helpful, and people took notice. Clementine felt self-empowered and desirous of going further. She attended conferences, formed networks, and learned more about community colleges' overall governance and the policies that guide them. Clementine also found herself attending board meetings and observing the process. Encouraged by her mentors, she applied for an Associate Dean of Instruction job at another college and got the position. This new job was a challenge because the administrative deans and faculty did not respect it. Her reforms were met with resistance from the division deans who felt they were outside her purview, which they thought was to monitor what they sent her. She met the challenge, which improved her problem-solving skills at an upper level. As she explained, "It was not how I felt going through it at the time and back then." These challenging experiences were to be many as she sought to learn the business of college administration. At the same school, she was later promoted to Assistant Dean of Instruction for staff development, grant writing, community services-adult learning, and outreach to high schools.

During her tenure and new-found growth and practical understanding, she experienced new leadership that was more informed, global, and less parochial in thought and behavior. Through new leadership, she was appointed acting dean for a sizeable academic division that put her in a line position for the first time. More specifically, she had faculty and staff reporting to her, whereas before, it was just a few classified people and no depth of responsibilities. Remaining in this position for nearly five years, Clementine's experience helped her grow and mature in ways she had not known before. She gained a credible reputation at the state level among her colleagues and was appointed to statewide committees and commissions, and most importantly, she started serving on accreditation visits. As she explains, "The experience was invaluable." Because of her tenure of nearly 15 years, she was recruited for her first big job as the Dean of Instruction and later as VP for Academic Affairs at a college in a large urban multi-college district, wherein she reported directly to the president of the college. After two and a half years on the job, the president who hired her was recruited to a more extensive job, and as luck and preparation intervened, she was appointed the acting president for a half year by the Chancellor of the district. Clementine's experiences throughout the system gave her the breadth, depth, and experience that resulted in her recruitment to serve as the CEO of a Community College District for more than 15 years before retiring from the district with distinction.

## LESSONS TO BE LEARNED

In looking at the above case study, let us observe how some American Association of Community Colleges (AACC) competencies are integrated into Clementine's journey. *Communication* is listed, as it helps to promote success across the organization and involves clear listening, speaking, and writing. It also helps to promote and enhance success, create stability, enhance transparency, and engenders a level of trust across the organization that extends into the community. *Experience* is another AACC competency that Clementine needed and became an essential next step for her to achieving the presidency. Thus, it is critical for aspirants not to dismiss any opportunity to learn something new or to take on a new challenge. In light of multiple experiences, it is thus essential to realize that all choices are good ones and that some, which on the surface appear unimportant and unrelated to the goal, are the ones that will be quite significant in the larger picture.

In the case study, Clementine mirrors the value of gaining "Depth and Breadth" of Experiences, albeit she was not always sure of the roles and, in some cases, the expectations of each new assignment. The president wears many hats and hears many voices throughout the organization, and must be prepared to be empathetic, open, and aware, with a knowledge base that comes from interacting with many perspectives, situations, and challenging circumstances. Accumulated experience is valuable, as it builds individual talent, interest, and desire. Similarly, having various experiences that are not necessarily tied to one area within higher education is immensely valuable. Advisedly, one should avoid falling into the one-size-fits-all regarding needed experience. It is best to get as much as one can and in as many areas as possible, keeping in mind what one is striving for and building on their experiences to serve the college more effectively.

An important lesson to take away from Clementine's experience fits into the AAACs competencies for presidents is Collaboration. Collaboration is essential for the overall success and well-being of the organization. It links to professionalism, as not all situations are attractively packaged or ripe for easy decision-making. In this context, the leader must model ethical behavior while upholding standards for herself and for others to see. One must first be what they want others to do. Only in that way is effective collaborative leadership possible.

A final essential role of the president is the ability to manage resources. It can be boosted by having a breadth of experience managing budgets and understanding how to work within their limitations while accomplishing the projected goals. It equitably and ethically sustains people, processes, information, and physical and financial assets to fulfill the community college's mission, vision, and goals. Clementine's experience through her range of experiences provided the skill sets needed to manage more complex budgets as she operated in the president's role and served in an advocacy role for the college's mission and goals.

In conclusion, the comparison of Clementine's journey to the AACC leadership competencies clearly shows a connection for success.

## REFERENCE

Jones, S. J., & Warnick, E. M. (2012). Attaining the first community college presidency: A case study of new presidents in Texas. *Community College Journal of Research and Practice*, 36, 229–232. doi:10.1080/10668926.2012.627808.

Part IV

# Competencies for the Future

Chapter Fifteen

# Guides to Building 21st-Century Competencies

Community college leadership competencies have been charted for over 100 years. As shown in this book, these competencies are time-stamped and often affiliated with corresponding educational reforms within the community college and socioeconomic and political changes within the country. This chapter compares the leadership competencies identified from associations, from the literature, and from the presidents interviewed for this book to build a composite profile of what new leaders need to consider in their professional development. A comparison of leadership competencies is shown in Table 15.1, and a more detailed listing of the President's personality and professional traits are compared in Table 15.2. It is important to note that a composite of these competencies cannot possibly match a single candidate.

## LEADERSHIP COMPETENCIES: A VIEW FROM THREE LENS

### According to Associations

In the early part of the 2000s, the American Association of Community Colleges (AACC) developed a set of leadership competencies and then used those competencies to support an industry of professional development programs. Essential for future leadership is that Boards of Trustees now frequently refer to these competencies for guidance on how they structure their president job announcements and how they communicate

**Table 15.1 Comparative Competencies**

| Competencies | Association | Literature | Interviews | Consultants |
|---|---|---|---|---|
| Commitment to student access | X | | X | |
| Strategic vision | X | X | X | X |
| Strategic decision-making process | | X | X | |
| Take risks | X | X | X | |
| Think beyond traditional ways | X | | X | |
| Entrepreneurialism | X | | | X |
| Institutional finance and budget | X | X | | |
| Fiscal resource management | X | | X | X |
| Fundraising | X | | | X |
| Community college advocacy | X | | | |
| Professionalism | X | X | | |
| Communication skills | X | X | X | X |
| Collaboration skills | X | X | X | |
| Technical skills | | X | | |
| Research skills | X | X | X | |
| Interpersonal competency skills | | X | | |
| Conflict resolution skills | | X | X | |
| Motivate people skills | | X | | |
| Encourage others to be creative | | X | X | |
| Know what it means to lead | | X | | |
| Passion, humility, and courage | | X | X | |
| Drive, grit, persistence, confidence | | X | X | |
| Ethical skills and honesty | | X | X | X |
| Balance multiple pressures | | X | X | |
| External relationship-building | | | X | X |
| Professional development | X | | X | |
| Networking | | X | X | |
| Balance work and work time | | | X | |
| Deal with intersectionality prejudice | | | X | |

to the hiring committee what they are looking for and expect in a leader. Key AACC competencies are summarized in Table 15.3.

Under the leadership of George Boggs, the AACC released the "A Competency Framework for Community College Leaders" (2005), which identified six essential leadership competencies. Influencing this Framework

Table 15.2 Changing Presidential Personalities Traits and Professional Traits

| | 1990s | 2000s | 2010s |
|---|---|---|---|
| **Prior Skills/Traits** | | | |
| Have a terminal degree | Vineyard (1993), Vaughan and Weisman (1998) | Schmidt (2008), Weltsch (2009) | Ellis and Garcia (2017) |
| Be a faculty | Vineyard (1993) | Weltsch (2009) | McNair (2016), Peters and Ryan (2015) |
| Work in student services | Vineyard (1993) | | |
| Degree in community college leadership or higher Education | McFarlin et al. (1999), McCarthy (1999) | Romano et al. (2009) | |
| Research and data analysis | | | Eckel and Kezar (2011), Achieving the Dream (2012), Bumphus (2015), Eddy (2013) |
| Publish – prestige economy | McFarlin et al. (1999) | | Blackmore and Kandiko (2011) |
| Participate in mentoring | Merriam and Thomas (1986) | | |
| Sociocultural, political and economic knowledge | | Plinske and Packard (2003) | Bonner (2013) |
| Specialized leadership training | Vaughan and Weisman (1998) | Boggs (2004), Eddy (2005) | Eddy (2018), Eddy et al. (2015), Strom et al. (2011), Reille and Kezar (2010) |
| Lifelong learning | Campbell and Leverty (1997) | Birnbaum an Umbach (2001), Casner-Lotto and Barrington (2006), Wallin (2002) | Ellis and Garcia (2017), Smerek (2010) |
| **Personality Skills/Trait** | | | |
| Intelligence | Duncan and Harlacher (1991) | Mumford et al. (2000), Boggs (2004), Geoff (2002) | Hayden and Jenkins (2015), AACC (2012), Ellis and Garcia (2017) |
| Drive and grit and self-direction | Duncan and Harlacher (1991) | | Bonner (2013), Hayden and Jenkins (2015), De Fruyt et al. (2015) |

| | 1990s | 2000s | 2010s |
|---|---|---|---|
| Passion | Portes (1998) | Birnbaum (2004), Myran et al. (2003) | Plinske and Packard (2010), Hayden and Jenkins (2015), Frost et al. (2011), McNair (2016) |
| Persistence | Duncan and Harlacher (1991) | | Bonner (2013), Hayden and Jenkins (2015) |
| Focused/committed | | Eddy and VanDerLinden (2006), Weisman and Vaughan (2002) | De Fruyt et al. (2015), Hayden and Jenkins (2015) |
| Fearless/courage/confident | Fisher and Tack (1998) | | O'Banion et al. (2011), Hayden and Jenkins (2015), Garza Mitchel and Cano-Monreal (2015) |
| Realistic | | Eddy and VanDerLinden (2006) | |
| Adaptability | | | Pellegrino and Hilton (2012) |
| Creativity | | | Markle (2012), O'Banion et al. (2011), Garza Mitchel and Cano-Monreal (2015) |
| Good people skills | Duncan and Harlacher (1991) | Mumford et al. (2000) | Burrus and Robert (2017) |
| Personal values/integrity/honesty/ethics | Leslie and Fretwell (1996), Duncan and Harlacher (1991) | Kezar and Eckel (2002), Casner-Lotto and Barrington (2006), Eddy (2003), Geoff (2002) | Eddy (2010b), Hornak and Garza Mitchell (2016), Hayden and Jenkins (2015), AACC (2012) |
| Motivation | | | Plinske and Packard (2010), Hayden and Jenkins (2015), Garza Mitchel and Cano-Monreal (2015), Blackmore and Kandiko (2011) |

| | 1990s | 2000s | 2010s |
|---|---|---|---|
| Heightened sensitivities/ awareness | | | Mathis and Roueche (2013) |
| Physical energy | Duncan and Harlacher (1991) | | Bonner (2013) |
| Critical thinking | Fisher and Tack (1998), Vaughan and Weisman (1998) | Casner-Lotto and Barrington (2006) | |
| Balance multiple priorities | | | Eddy (2010), Hayden and Jenkins (2015), Bonner (2013) |
| Cultural sensitivity | | Casner-Lotto and Barrington (2006) | |
| Intersectionality lived experiences: race/ gender | | Amey et al. (2002) | Coate and Howson (2016) |
| **Professionalism** | | | |
| Career pathways, communication skills (oral and written) | Marlier and Bragg (1983), Wessel and Keim (1994), Townsend and Bassoppo-Moyo (1997) | Amey and VanDerLinden (2002), Birnbaum and Umbach (2001), Madsen (2006), Markle (2012), Casner-Lotto and Barrington (2006), Boggs (2004), AACC (2005), Plinske and Packard (2003) | Mathis and Roueche (2013), Eddy and Kirby (2020), Eddy (2010), Garza Mitchel and Cano-Monreal (2015), Plinske and Packard (2010), AACC (2012), Markle (2012), Rios et al. (2020) |
| Frame meaning to communicate | | | Eddy (2010) |
| Technical competence | Townsend and Bassoppo-Moyo (1997), Weisman and Vaughan's (1998) | | Eckel and Kezar (2011), AACC (2013) |
| Know – higher education | Fisher and Tack (1998), Vaughan and Weisman (1998) | | |

| | 1990s | 2000s | 2010s |
|---|---|---|---|
| Know – budget management | | Wallin (2002), Lambert (2008), Plinske and Packard (2003) | Tarker (2019), Bumphus (2014), Eddy (2013), Eckel and Kezar (2011), AACC (2012) |
| Know – curricular reform-student completion | | | Parker (2019) |
| Know – organizational behavior skills | | Boggs (2004), Sullivan (2001), Goff (2002), AACC (2005) | Ellis and Garcia (2017) |
| Know – managerial skills and time management skills | | Mitchell and Eddy (2008), Anderson et al. (2002), Geoff (2002), Wallin (2002) | McArdle (2013), Peters and Ryan (2015), Binkley (2012) |
| Know – decision-making skills | Campbell and Leverty (1997), Harris (1994) | Eddy (2003) | Hornak and Garza Mitchell (2016), Eddy (2010) |
| Know – political business insight; academic capitalism | | Sullivan (2001, 2004) | Ellis and Garcia (2017) |
| Know-how to work in political minefields | | | Eddy and Kirby (2020) |
| Know – technology and social media | Weisman and Vaughan (1998) | Wallin (2002), Sullivan (2001), Lambert (2008) | Eddy (2013) |
| Know political advocacy: local and state | | Wallin (2002) | Eckel and Kezar (2011), AACC (2015), Ellis and Garcia (2017) |
| Contextual competence | Townsend and Bassoppo-Moyo (1997) | Casner-Lotto and Barrington (2006) | |
| Strategic thinking and planning and problem-solving | Campbell and Leverty (1997) | Gumport (2003), Eddy (2005), Myran et al. (2003), Hassan (2008) | Eddy and Kirby (2020), Burrus and Robert (2017), Sutin et al. (2011) |
| Conflict resolution | | Wallin (2002) | Mathis and Roueche (2013), Eddy and Kirby (2020) |
| Take calculated risks | Fisher and Tack (1998) | | |

| | 1990s | 2000s | 2010s |
|---|---|---|---|
| Take general risk-taking | Gumport (2003), Weisman and Vaughan (1998), Fisher and Tack (1998) | Aspen Institute (2004) | O'Brien (2019) |
| Entrepreneurialism and fundraising | Slaughter (1993) | Aspen Institute, (2004), Wallin (2002), AACC (2005), Gumport (2003) | AACC (2012, 2015), McNair (2016), Jacobs and Worth (2019), Oakley and Bynum (2017) |
| Motivational skills | Campbell and Leverty (1997) | Sullivan (2004), Wiseman and Vaughan (2002) | Eddy et al. (2016) |
| Encourage people to think differently and creatively | Levin (1995), Fisher and Tack (1998) | Kabala and Bailey (2001) | Sutin e al. (2011) |
| Group relations/ collaborations building and consensus buy-in | Hammons and Keller (1990), Campbell and Leverty (1997), Weisman and Vaughan (1998), Fisher and Tack (1998), Tack (1991) | Sullivan (2001), Casner-Lotto and Barrington (2006), Sullivan (2001), Goff (2002), Goff (2002), Boggs (2004), AACC (2005), Wallin (2002), Budros (2002) | Eddy and Kirby (2020), AACC (2012), Boggs and McPhail (2016), Eddy and Khwaja (2019) |
| Interactive problem-solving; group participation | | | Eddy (2010), Grasmick et al. (2012), De Fruyt et al. (2015) |
| Talk the walk | | | Eddy and Kirby (2020) |
| Respect is more important than being liked | Fisher and Tack (1998) | | |
| Be authoritative, not collegial | Fisher and Tack (1998) | Wallin (2002) | |
| Plan actions and speech, do not be spontaneous | Fisher and Tack (1998) | | Eddy (2010) |
| Respond in real time | | Eddy and VanDerLinden (2006) | |
| Work long hours | Fisher and Tack (1998) | | Bonner (2013) |

| | 1990s | 2000s | 2010s |
|---|---|---|---|
| **Leadership Styles** | | | |
| Transformative leadership | | Astin and Astin (2000), Romano et al. (2009) | Parker (2019), AACC (2013), O'Banion (2019) |
| Lead change/change agent | Campbell and Leverty (1997), Tack (1991) | Wallin (2002), Aspen Institute (2004), Sullivan (2004), Mumford et al. (2000), Astin and Astin (2000), Boggs (2003), Eddy (2003) | Boggs and McPhail (2016), Mathis and Roueche (2013), McNair et al. (2011), Cloud (2010) |
| Networked leadership | | | Eddy and Kirby (2020), Eckel and Kezar (2011), AACC (2013) |
| Visionary-based leadership | Fisher and Tack (1998) | Binder (2000), Aspen Institute (2004) | Grasmick et al. (2012), Eddy (2010), McNair (2016) |
| Participatory leadership | | | Grasmick et al. (2012) |
| Culture of innovation | | | O'Banion et al. (2011) |
| Push the envelope | | | Bumphus (2015) |
| Lead without authority | | Garza Mitchell and Eddy (2008) | |
| Good "fit" for the role | | | Denny (2020) |
| Gendered leadership styles | | | Eddy and Khwaja (2019) |
| Diversity and equity in leaders and decision-making: racial, ethnic, and gender leaders | | McKenney and Cejda (2001) | McNair et al. (2011), Martinez and Herney (2017), Bell et al. (2018), Garza Mitchell and Garcia (2018), Eddy and Khwaja (2019), Ellis and Garcia (2017) |
| Learning-centered: get results | | | Boggs and McPhail (2016), Mathis and Roueche (2013) |

were essential presidential leadership competencies outlined by the Aspen Institute (2004, 2013) in the document "Crisis and Opportunity: Aligning the Community College Presidency with Student Success." These documents specifically linked leadership to maximizing student achievement and success. In 2013, the AACC revisited the Competencies Framework

Table 15.3 Association Competencies

| Time | Competencies |
|---|---|
| 2004 (Aspen) | 1. A deep commitment to student access and success<br>2. Willingness to take significant risks to advance student success<br>3. The ability to create lasting change within the college<br>4. Having a strong, broad strategic vision for the college and its students, reflected in external partnerships<br>5. An ability to raise and allocate resources in ways aligned to student success |
| 2005 (AACC) | 1. Organizational strategy<br>2. Resource management<br>3. Communication<br>4. Collaboration<br>5. Community college advocacy<br>6. Professionalism<br>7. Participatory leadership |
| 2015 (AACC) | 1. Institutional finance<br>2. Research<br>3. Fundraising<br>4. Resource management |
| 2020 (AACC) | 1. Thinking beyond traditional ways of delivering programs and services to align with changing institutional structures and missions<br>2. Entrepreneurialism<br>3. Career progression to improve proficiencies<br>4. Hero leader |

and then, in 2015, under the guidance of Walter Bumphus, created the Emerging Leaders profiles. In these documents, new competencies were added to help leaders to deal with decreasing federal and state budgets, student demands for lower tuition, and linking educational reform to data-driven decisions. Finally, in 2020, under the leadership of Walter Bumphus, AACC revised the Competency Framework to reflect current issues of the day with a focus to help leaders deal with a changing environment resulting from plunging US global educational rankings, issues of equity, poverty, and systemic racism.

The 2020 AACC competencies focused on the president's willingness to take a risk, develop and then advance a strategic vision, embrace fundraising, know resource management, be a collaborator and effective communicator, use research skills to ground decisions, and be entrepreneurial. Relevant competencies also questioned leadership that keeps the status quo a viable alternative for aspiring community college CEOs. These competencies were designed to respond to an environment where social justice issues are front and center, where openly carrying firearms threatens the populace, and political discourse lines up as either red or blue with no room for discussion or compromise. It is where job inequality is growing for some even with proper credentialing, where systemic racism hinders student access and success, and where discussion on the value of the degree is gaining momentum, as more and more people in pursuit of it become debt-ridden. It is exacerbated by the COVID-19 pandemic and the George Floyd death that has turned the world upside down.

## According to the Literature

In the literature, authors identify specific leadership competencies that mostly align with the times they were published. The leadership competencies can be categorized into those focusing on personality traits and those focusing on professional traits. Table 15.2 provides examples from the literature on how the focus of these competencies changed over time.

### Personality Traits

In the 1990s, personality traits of integrity, persistence, and passion grounded what was expected in community college presidents (Kirkland & Ratcliff, 1994). These traits were believed to influence professional decisions, especially those about commitment to one's vision and ability to undertake calculated risk rather than spontaneous decision-making (Fisher & Tack, 1998). Similarly, other personality traits were seen as essential in supporting professionalism, such as having good people skills to enable the president to build and sustain collaborative groups (Hammons & Keller, 1990). Townsend and Bassoppo-Moyo (1997) summarized the needed competencies as (a) contextual competency, (b) technical competency, and (c) communication skills competency. The foundation for transformational leadership was also introduced (Roueche, 1989). The personality traits helped to drive the leader's image as a hero whose decisive actions resulted in substantial changes for the institution (Sullivan, 2001). Embedded within the hero construct were implicit masculine and White leadership traits that reinforced inequities in leadership styles and expectations of women and leaders of color (Eddy & Khwaja, 2019).

In the 2000s, the personality traits that were favored by authors in the 1990s were repeated. In part, this continuity was linked to presidential pathways that came from within ranks (Ellis & Garcia, 2017; Mitchell & Eddy, 2008; Wiseman & Vaughan, 2007) and that mirrored mentors' leadership styles. As in each generation, subtle changes in successful leadership emerged. New to the millennium presidents were a valued personality trait of motivating others and seeing oneself as a leader (Amey et al., 2002; Sullivan, 2001). In the 2000s, the leaders as a hero image were challenged by a new image of the "servant" leader who served the institution (Grasmick et al., 2012). New competencies of communication, collaboration, and outreach were influenced by a new generation of mostly White women presidents defining their leadership styles. Another critical aspect of the 2000s was that due to the high turnover in positions, AACC and other associations started reexamining career pathways (AACC, 2005; Schmitz, 2008; Weltsch, 2009). In this context, the trustee's voice was included, as the trustees started to define what they felt were essential skillsets (AACC/ ACCT, 2015; Hassan, 2008). The literature also began to acknowledge a new professional competency called "just-in-time responses" that would allow leaders to respond quickly in periods of economic crisis and dramatic changes in higher education resulting from globalization and technology explosions (Eddy & VanDerLinden, 2006). Finally, a new focus on entrepreneurial skills became important as profit-oriented decisions were becoming critical to the institution (Gumport, 2003).

In the 2010s, the desired personality traits changed to meet the demands of the new decade. While some traits remained the same from the previous generation, the new leadership style of being a transformative leader required personalities of grit (Bonner, 2013), strong communication skills (Mathis & Roueche, 2013), strategic thinking (Eddy & Kirby, 2020), and the ability to use vision to ground change (Grasmick et al., 2012). Hayden and Jenkins (2015) summarized that exceptional leaders have eight ordinary virtues: (a) courage, (b) hope, (c) humility, (d) perseverance, (e) charity, (f) honesty, (g) balance, and (h) wisdom. Even though feminine leadership traits persisted, the male-dominated leader's reemergence as a hero once again took root.

### Professional Traits

In the 2000s, the literature identified four leadership constructs. The first was the transformative leader (Tarker, 2019), the second was leadership in promoting a culture of innovation (O'Banion, 2019), the third was a reimagining of the servant leadership role (Stauffer & Maxwell, 2020), and last was the leadership to improve student success (Kanter & Armstrong, 2019). The reimagined skills were built upon the 1990s "good manager" styles (Goff, 2002), which included knowledge of managing fiscal resources, effectively building strong teams to achieve goals, and skills to bring a vision to life. Philosophically, discussions arose as to what it meant to be an agent of change and an agent of stability (Boggs, 2003; Eddy, 2005; Hassan et al., 2010). In the 2010s, the preferred competencies shifted to being able to balance multiple pressures (Bonner, 2013), to plan a career, but be open to unexpected opportunities (Peters & Ryan, 2015), to anticipate and work within political minefields (Eddy & Kirby, 2020), to apply "entrepreneurial" thinking (AACC, 2020), and to build a culture of innovation (O'Banion et al., 2011). In turn, these skills demanded that skills of research, data analysis and assessment (Binkley et al., 2012), the skills of problem-solving (De Fruyt et al., 2015), and the capacity to foster active and broad-based participation in campus decision-making processes (Denny, 2020; Grasmik et al., 2012). Eddy (2010) identified three essential competencies presidents needed to adopt: (a) visionary framing to focus on future possibilities; (b) step-by-step framing to outline chronological activities; and (c) connective framing to emphasize the importance of dialogue and collaborative learning. Scholars concurred that especially during times of crisis, decision-making expands to focus on the ability of the president to make decisions that are in alignment with a college's mission, vision, and values, but that are equally highly influenced by the presidents' values (Hornak & Garza Mitchell, 2016). Related is an increased importance placed on the "prestige economy," emphasizing the need to publish to demonstrate one's leadership authority (Blackmore & Kandiko, 2011; Coate & Howson, 2016). Steffens et al. (2014) called the social identity management model the intersection of personality and professional traits.

During the 2010s, literature also focused on masculine and feminist leadership styles to show underlying inequities. Similar discussions that identified specific leadership styles were based on race, mostly focused on increasing numbers (Vaughan, 1989). Only recently has there been an attempt to chart unique leadership styles (Eddy, 2018). However, much of the literature has documented differences in gender-specific leadership traits. Masculine traits were seen as those that supported power, such as confidence, willingness to face challenges, preparation, and being able to use power to control others in what has been referred to as the leader hero (Acker, 1990; Eddy & Khwaja, 2019). Feminine leadership traits focused on organization and included participatory leadership, networking, connectivity, and intercultural competence (Eddy, 2012) that would enable the leader to empower others and thereby support changes within the institution (Amey, 2013). Although 50% of the presidents were women by the end of the decade, inequities are maintained as women presidents continue to be judged relative to the masculine norm (Howard & Gagliardi, 2018). Moreover, many of the feminine style competencies echoed in the AACC 2013 Competencies favored by women and presidents of color lost their appeal in the late 2010s. Notably, in the AACC 2020 Competencies Framework, many of the preferred competencies echo back to traditional male-style competencies that are now increasingly favoring traditional authoritative positions (Eddy & Khwaja, 2019).

Finally, within the literature is what is referred to as 21st-century skills (Burrus et al., 2013; Duckworth & Yeager, 2015; Pellegrino & Hilton, 2012; Rios et al., 2020). The 21st-century skills define leadership traits in terms of cognitive skills (nonroutine problem-solving, critical thinking, metacognition), interpersonal skills (social), and intrapersonal skills (emotional, self-regulatory). Nevertheless, grounded in 21st-century skills are skills from the past, which continue to place high importance on oral and written communication, collaboration, and problem-solving skills.

## Presidential Search Consultant Survey

The connection of competencies outlined in the literature has relevance to those honored by trustees in their selection process for future presidents. The AACC Competencies for Community College Leaders (2012) was a research study of the opinions of eight search consultants, who collectively conducted more than 500 community college presidential searches. These consultants identified the following skills as the most important: (a) fiscal management, (b) fundraising, (c) external relationship-building, (d) communication, and (e) ethical and risk-averse behaviors. The consultants concluded that these skills would enable the future president to (1) manage and find new revenues and expenditures; (2) build relationship with external players for new economic development opportunities; (3) master communication to be useful internally and externally to share the college's mission, vision, and goals; and (4) maintain ethical behavior to ensure the president will avoid issues and activities that could be an embarrassment to the organization. Across the board, some of these statements are still used in job announcements in 2020.

## Confirmed by Buttimer Awardees and Sitting Presidents

The Buttimer awardees and the Sitting Presidents confirmed the importance of the competencies suggested by AACC and those found in the literature. These presidents agreed with the literature that presidents need to be creative, caring, have a passion, and have a vision. They also agreed with the AACC competencies to base decisions on research and data, be entrepreneurial, and use their career progression to improve proficiencies. One of the competencies most mentioned by both the Buttimer and the Sitting Presidents is building a personalized leadership skill set that they confirmed are best developed via attendance in AACC-sponsored professional development training programs. Like the literature, the presidents in the study conducted for this book, all confirmed the importance of fiscal resource management, communication skills, and balancing multiple pressures.

Both the Buttimer recipients and the Sitting Presidents identified competencies that were not found in association or literature competencies. The Buttimer recipients, many of whom were presidents in the late 1990s and 2000s, saw themselves as caring but did not see themselves as heroes. The skill sets that they defined as essential were precisely those that embodied the leader and a hero construct. While both presidents favored prescriptive problem-solving styles, they also supported creative choices that challenged the institution. The Sitting Presidents, who reflect current practices of the 2010s, applied transformative leadership styles but grounded those choices in their sense of duty to change lives. While they labeled their purpose as being servant-leader, they still favored directed leadership styles of the "good manger" found in the 1990s.

The more recent Buttimer awardees and the Sitting Presidents favored the new AACC (2020) competencies that embodied research as a strategy to ground decision-making. Many also stressed the importance of creativity to ground change-focused problem-solving. While AACC (2020) focused on entrepreneurial change, all of the presidents interviewed for this book did not mention entrepreneurialism as a style or leadership quality. It is interesting to note that few of these presidents specifically talked about student success in terms of their leadership styles, and none talked about championing pedagogical or curriculum reforms that would be central in the learning paradigm (Boggs, 2019). Another notable difference is that none of the presidents mentioned emphasized technological skills, in contrast to the AACC competencies and the literature, which labeled these skills of great importance.

Finally, the presidents interviewed for this book shared a unique focus that is not found in the AACC competencies and minimized in the literature. One unique focus of the presidents was their need to understand their motivation for becoming a president and then critically assessing how that motivation grounds their decision-making strategies. Another unique competency mentioned by the Sitting Presidents was the need to balance work and self-time. Eddy and Khwaja (2019) suggest that the emphasis on being married enabled White male presidents to focus on the college as their wives took care of their personal life. With the diversification of the presidency, as shown in our sample, wives were substituted by husbands in some contexts. In other contexts, the balance of work and home were emphasized instead. The Sitting Presidents also mentioned the final unique competency: the need to effectively deal with biases and prejudices based on race, ethnicity, and LGBTQI+ status. The Buttimer presidents added biases from former coworkers and from being young. These are biases and prejudices not mentioned in most of the literature.

## BUILDING COMPETENCIES FOR THE NEXT GENERATION

As community colleges evolve, new competencies will be required for future presidents' role, function, and leadership. The future sociocultural and economic challenges will continue to influence the presidency, especially in leadership choices. It will include participatory governance, a decline in government funding, scarcity of resources, and increased accountability. Significantly, access, support for students who may be underprepared, international education, virtual learning, increasing technology costs, expanded budget demands, recruiting and onboarding staff, demographic shifts, and private sector creep lead to increased competition and institutional racism. There is rapid turnover in community college leadership; there is an unprecedented opportunity to reconsider community college leadership through fresh lenses to address these challenges. Nevertheless, at the same time, and perhaps most importantly, it remains ones' values and knowledge that are the most important in guiding decision-making strategies. Finally, it is the need to seek to counter gendered and racial inequities actively.

While the competencies mentioned above are essential, it is necessary to emphasize that the leaders of tomorrow must also maintain the skill sets of the past in being authentic, visionary, passionate, disciplined, intentional, curious, and to possess the ability to work on self while simultaneously serving the team for the greater public good. Future leaders will need to have the courage to face their weaknesses and have challenging and critically focused conversations with themselves to build sensemaking about where they need to grow and change. Finally, the future educational challenges will demand that presidents possess on-time leadership competencies that embody those defined by the associations, the literature, and the presidents interviewed for this book.

In summary, the essential qualities for emerging leadership, identified by association leaders, by academics, by the Buttimer Award recipients, and by the Sitting Presidents, include a set of clear, positive, and rationally defensible values to rely on when making decisions. Moving into the next decade, future presidents will need to have the courage to focus on quality, a willingness to take calculated risks to capitalize on new opportunities. They must have the ability to balance competing, often consuming, demands of their work and their personal lives. In 1991, Tack suggested that higher education leaders of the future will have to include other constituencies from across campuses in the decision-making process to empower those with whom they work and to use all their talents constructively to ensure organizational success. Today, we call that being change agents informed by Goleman's (2006) qualities that refers to emotional intelligence. Notably, an effective leader will be one who can affect change through democratic consensus, obtain particularly good results from collaborative groups while maintaining consistently high morale, and a feeling of individual accomplishment. However, most importantly, tomorrow's leaders need to have a moral compass in which decisions foster equity and help move the college, the students, and the community into social change. In effect, the "people skills" are of the highest order in which the president raises the voices of a diverse team of people with different skills, knowledge, abilities, age, experience, race, ethnicity, and gender to meet the organizations' desired visions and goals.

## REFERENCES

Acker, J. (1990). Hierarchies, jobs, bodies: A theory of gendered organizations. *Gender and Society*, 4, 139–158. doi:10.1177/089124390004002002.

American Association of Community Colleges (AACC). (2005). *Competency framework for community college leaders*. http://www.aacc.nche.edu/competency_framework/pdf.

American Association of Community Colleges (AACC). (2012). *Competencies for community college leaders*. https://www.aacc.nche.edu/content/uploads/2017/09/AACC.

American Association of Community Colleges (AACC). (2013). *Competencies for community college leaders*. Second Edition. AACC. www.aacc.nche.edu/newsevents/Events/leadershipsuite/Documents/AACC/CoreCompetencies/web.pdf.

American Association of Community Colleges (AACC). (2015). Emerging Leaders. Leadership institute documents. www.aacc.nche.edu/newsevents/Emergingleaders/leadershipsuiteDocuments/AACC.

American Association of Community Colleges (AACC). (2020). *Competencies for community college leaders*. Third Edition. www.aacc.nche.edu/publications-news/aacc-competencies-for-community-college-leaders/.

American Association of Community Colleges and the Association of Community College Trustees (ACCT). (2015). *Thriving in the community college presidency*. www.aacc.nche.edu/newsevents/Events/leadershipsuite/Documents/CC%20Presidency%20Meeting%202012-13.pdf.

Amey, M. J. (2013). Leadership: Community college transitions. In *Understanding community colleges*. Edited by J. S. Levin, & S. T. Kater (pp. 135–152). Routledge.

Amey, M., VanDerLinden, K., & Brown, D. (2002). Perspectives on community college leadership: Twenty years in the making. *Community College Journal of Research and Practice*, 26(7–8), 573–589. doi:10.1080/10668920276018 1805.

Anderson, P., Murray, J. P., & Olivarez, A. (2002). The managerial roles of public community college Chief Academic Officers. *Community College Review*, 30(2), 1–26. https://doi.org/10.1177/009155210203000201

Aspen Institute. (2004). Crisis and opportunity: Aligning the community college presidency with student success. www.aspeninstitute.org/publications/crisis-opportunity-aligning-community-college-presidency-student-success/.

Aspen Institute. (2013). Crisis and opportunity: Aligning the community college presidency with student success. www.aspeninstitute.org/publications/crisis-opportunity-aligning-community-college-presidency-student-success.

Astin, A. W. & Astin, H. S. (2000). *Leadership reconsidered: Engaging higher education in social change*. W.K. Kellogg Foundation. http://eric.ed.gov/?id=ED444437

Bell, K., Donaghue, J., & Gordon, A. (2018). Collaborative leadership: Advancing diversity, equity, and comprehensive internationalization in higher education. Diversity Abroad White Paper

Binder, F. M. (2000). So you want to be a college president?" COSMOS Journal. www./smosclub.org/journals/2000/binder.html

Binkley, M., Erstrad, O., Herman, J. Raizen, S., Ripley, M., Miller-Ricci, M., & Rumble, M. (2012). Defining 21st century skills. In *Assessment and teaching of 21st-century skills*. Edited by B. Griffin, & E. C. McGraw (pp. 17–66). Springer.

Birnbaum, R. (2004). The end of shared governance: Looking ahead or looking back. New Directions for Higher Education, (127), 5-22. Jossey-Bass.

Birnbaum, R., & Umbach, P. D. (2001). Scholar, steward, spanner, stranger: The four career paths of college presidents. The Review of Higher Education, 24(3), 203–217.

Blackmore, P., & Kandiko, C. B. (2011). Motivation in academic life: A prestige economy. *Research in Post-Compulsory Education*, 16(4), 399–411. doi: 10.1080/13596748.2011.626971.

Boggs, G. R. (2003). Leadership context for the twenty-first century. *New Directions for Community Colleges*, 123(Fall), 15–25.

Boggs, G. R. (2004). The leader as an agent of change and stability. Paper presentation: The American Association of Community Colleges Future Leader Institute in Long Beach, California [July].

Boggs, G. R. (2019). The learning paradigm. *In 13 ideas that are transforming the community college world*. Edited by T. U. O'Banion (pp. 33–51). Roman & Littlefield.

Boggs, G. R., & McPhail, C. J. (2016). Practical leadership in community colleges: Navigating today's challenges. John Wiley and Sons / Jossey-Bass.

Bonner, B. J. (2013). Leading the charge: A multiple case study of presidential perceptions of essential leadership characteristics for the 21st-century community college. [Doctoral Dissertation]. University of Nebraska at Lincoln.

Burrus, J., Jackson, T., Xi, N., & Steinberg, J. (2013). *Identifying the most important 21st-century workforce competencies: An analysis of the Occupational Information Network (O*NET) (ETS RR-13-21)*. Educational Testing Service.

Burrus, J., Mattern, K. D., Naemi, B. D., & Roberts, R. D. (2017). Establishing an international standards framework and action research agenda for workplace readiness and success. In Building better students: Preparation for the workforce. Edited by J. Golubovich, R. Su, S.B. Robbins. (pp. 303–338). Oxford University Press.

Campbell, D. F. & Leverty, L. H. (1997). Developing and selecting leaders for the 21st century. *Community College Journal*, 67, 34-36.

Casner-Lotto, J. & Barrington, L. (2006). *Are they really ready to work? Employers' perspectives on the basic knowledge and applied skills of new entrants to the 21st century US workforce*. Partnership for 21st Century Skills

Coate, K., & Howson, C. K. (2016). Indicators of esteem: Gender and prestige in academic work. *British Journal of Sociology of Education*, 37(4), 567–585. doi:10.1080/01425692.2014.955082.

De Fruyt, F., Wille, B., & John, O. P. (2015). Employability in the 2st century: Complex (interactive) problem-solving and other essential skills. *Industrial and Organizational Psychology*, 8(2), 276–281.

Denny, F. (2020). What I wish I'd known – Academic leadership in the UK, lessons for the next generation. *SRHE News Blog*. April 14. https://wp.me/p3XKMx-vO.

Duckworth, A. L., & Yeager, D. S. (2015). Measurement matters: Assessing personal qualities other than cognitive ability for educational purposes. *Educational Researcher*, 44, 237–251.

Duncan, A. H. & Harlacher, E. L. (1991). The twenty-first-century executive leader. *Community College Review*, 18(4) 39-47.

Duree, C. (2007). The challenge of the community college presidency in the new millennium: Pathways, preparation, competencies, and leadership programs needed to survive. [Unpublished doctoral dissertation]. Iowa State University.

Eckel, P. D., Cook, B. J. & King, J. E. (2009). *The CAO census: A national profile of chief academic officers*. American Council on Education.

Eddy, P. L. (2003). Sensemaking on campus: How community college presidents frame change. *Community College Review*, 27, 452-471. https://doi.oor/10.1080/713838185

Eddy, P. L. (2005). Framing the role of leader: How community college presidents construct their leadership. *Community College Journal of Research and Practice*, 29(9/10), 705–727.

Eddy, P. L. (2008). Leading gracefully: Gendered leadership at community colleges. In *Women in academic leadership*. Edited by D. R. Dean, S. J. Bracken, & J. K. Allen (pp. 8–30). Stylus.

Eddy, P. L. (2010). *Community college leadership: A multidimensional model for leading change*. Stylus.

Eddy, P. L. (2012). Developing leaders: The role of competencies in rural community colleges. *Community College Review*, 41, 20–43. doi:10.1177/0091552112471557.

Eddy, P. L. (2018). Expanding the leadership pipeline in community colleges: Fostering racial equity. *Teachers College Record*, 120(14), 1–18.

Eddy, P. L., & Khwaja, T. (2019). What happened to re-visioning community college leadership? A 25-year retrospective. *Community College Review*, 47(1), 53–78. doi:10.1177/0091552118818742.

Eddy, P. L., & Kirby, E. (2020). *Leading for tomorrow: A primer for succeeding in higher education leadership*. Rutgers University Press.

Eddy, P. L., & VanDerLinden, K. E. (2006). Emerging definitions of leadership in higher education: New visions of leadership or same old "hero" leader? *Community College Review*, 34(1), 5–26. doi:10.1177/0091552106289703.

Eddy, P. L., Garza Mitchell, R. And Amey, M. J. (2016). Leading from the middle. *Chronicle of Higher Education* 68(15), A48.

Eddy, P. L., Sydow, D., Alfred, R., & Garza Mitchell, R. (2015). *Developing tomorrow's leaders: Contexts, consequences, & competencies*. Community College Series: Rowman & Littlefield and ACCT.

Ellis, M. M., & Garcia, L. (2017). *Generation X presidents leading community colleges: New challenges, new leaders*. Rowan & Littlefield.

Fisher, J. L., & Tack, M. W. (eds.) (1998). *Leaders on leadership: The college presidency* (Vol. 61). Jossey-Bass.

Frost, R., Raspiller, E. T. & Sygielski, J.J. (2011). The role of leadership: Leaders' practice in financing transformation. In *Increasing effectiveness of the community college financial model: A global perspective for the global economy*. Edited by S.E. Sutin, D. Derrico, R.L. Raby & E.J. Valeau.(pp. 49-65). Palgrave.

Garza Mitchell, R. L. & Cano-Monreal, G. L. (2015). Strategic planning for new presidents: Developing an entrance plan. *Community College Journal of Research and Practice* 39(2), 113-121.

Garza Mitchell, R. L. & Eddy, P. L. (2008). In the middle: Career pathway of midlevel community college leaders. *Community College Journal of Research and Practice* 32(10), 793-811. https://doi.org/10.1080/10668920802325739

Goff, D. G. (2002). Community college presidency: What are the challenges to be encountered and the traits to be successful? ERIC Document Reproduction Service No. ED476 681.

Goleman, D. (2006). *Emotional intelligence.* Bantam Books.

Grasmick, L., Davies, T., & Harbour, C. (2012). Participative leadership: Perspectives of community college presidents. *Community College Journal of Research and Practice*, 36(2), 67–80. doi:10.1080/10668920802421496.

Gumport, P. J. (2003). The demand-response scenario: Perspectives of community college presidents. *The Annals of the American Academy of Political and Social Science*, 586, 38–61.

Hammons, J., & Keller, L. (1990). Competencies and personal characteristics of future community college presidents. *Community College Review*, 18(3) 34–41.

Hassan, A. M. (2008). The Competencies for community college leaders: Community college presidents' and trustee board chairpersons' perspectives. [Unpublished Doctoral Dissertation]. University of Southern Florida.

Hassan, A. M., Dellow, D. A., & and Jackson, R. J. (2010). The AACC leadership competencies: Parallel views from the top. *Community College Journal of Research and Practice*, 34(1), 180–198.

Hayden, N. K., & Jenkins, R. (2015). *9 Virtues of exceptional leaders – Unlocking your leadership potential.* Deeds.

Hornak, A. M., & Garza Mitchell, R. L. (2016). Changing times, complex decisions. *Community College Review*, 44(2), 119–194. doi:10.1177/0091552116629548.

Howard, E., & Gagliardi, J. (2018). Leading the way to parity: Preparation, persistence, and the role of women presidents. ACE Center for Policy, Research, and Strategy (CPRS). www.acenet.edu/news-room/Pages/Leading-the-Way-to-Parity.aspx.

Kabala, T. S. & Bailey, G. M. (2001). A new perspective on community college presidents: Results of a national study. *Community College Journal of Research and Practice* 25(6), p 793–804.

Kanter, M., & Armstrong, A. (2019). The college promise: Transforming the lives of community college students. *In 13 ideas that are transforming the community college world.* Edited by T. U. O'Banion (pp. 63–85). Roman & Littlefield.

Kezar A., Eckel P. D. (2002). Examining the institutional transformation process: The importance of sensemaking, interrelated strategies, and balance. *Research in Higher Education*, 43, 295–328.

Kirkland, T. P., & Ratcliff, J. L. (1994). When community colleges change their presidents. *Community College Review*, 21(4), 3–13.

Leslie D. W., Fretwell E. K. (1996). *Wise moves in hard times: Creating and managing resilient colleges and universities.* Jossey-Bass.

Levin, J. S. (1995). The community college presidency: Conditions and factors of impact on an institution. *Community College Journal of Research and Practice*, 19(5), 411–422.

McArdle, M. (2013). The next generation of community college leaders. Community College Journal of Research and Practice, 37(11), 851–863. https://doi-org/10.1080/10668926.2010.482483

McCarthy, M. (1999). The evolution of educational leadership preparation programs. In Handbook of Research on Educational Administration, 2nd ed. Edited by J. Murphy & K. S. Louis, (pp. 119–139). Jossey-Bass.

McFarlin, C. & Ebbers, L. (1998). Preparation factors common in outstanding community college presidents. Michigan Community College Journal, 4(1), 33–47.

McFarlin, C. H., Crittenden, B. J., & Ebbers, L. H. (1999). Background factors common among outstanding community college presidents. Community College Review, 27(3), 19–31.

McKenney, C. & Cejda, B. (2001). The Career Path and Profile of Women Chief Academic Officers in Public Community Colleges. Advancing Women in Leadership Journal.

McNair, D, E. (2016). Deliberate disequilibrium: Preparing for a community college presidency. Community College Review 43(1), 72–88.

McNair, D. E., Duree, C. A., & Ebbers, L. (2011). If I Knew Then What I Know Now: Using the Leadership Competencies developed by the American Association of Community Colleges to prepare community college presidents. Community College Review, 39(1), 3–25.

Markle, R., Brenneman, M., Jackson, T., Burus, J., & Robbins, S. (2013). Synthesizing frameworks of higher education student learning outcomes. Educational Testing Service.

Martinez, T. Jr. & Herney, S. A. (2017). NCCHC is filling leadership pipeline. Community College Week. April 24(4), p. 16.

Mathis, M. B., & Roueche, J. E. (2013, June 24). POV: Preparation of future leaders takes on new urgency. *Community College Week*. www.ccweek.com.

Merriam, S. B. & Thomas, T. K. (1986). The role of mentoring in the career development of community college presidents. Community/Junior College Quarterly, 10, 177–191.

Mitchell, R. L. G., & Eddy, P. L. (2008). In the middle: Career pathways of mid-level community college leaders. *Community College Journal of Research and Practice*, 32(10), 793–811. doi:10.1080/10668920802325739.

Mumford, M. D., Zaccaro, S. J., Harding, F. D., Jacobs, T. O., & Fleishman, E. A. (2000). Leadership skills for a changing world: Solving complex social problems. The Leadership Quarterly, 11(1), 11–35. https://doi.org/10.1016/S1048-9843(99)00041-7

Myran, G., Bakers, G. A., Simone, B., & Zeiss, T. (2003). Leadership Strategies for Community College Executives. American Association of Community Colleges.

O'Banion, T. (2019). *13 Ideas that are transforming the community college world.* Rowman and Littlefield.

O'Banion, T., Weidner, L., & Wilson, C. (2011). Creating a culture of innovation in the community college. *Community College Journal of Research and Practice*, 35(6), 470–483. doi:10.1080/10668926.2010.515508.

Pellegrino, J. W., & Hilton, M. L. (2012). *Education for life and work: Developing transferable knowledge and skills in the 21st century.* National Academy of Sciences.

Peters, K., & Ryan, M. (2015). *Motivating and developing leaders in Higher Education.* Report commissioned by the Leadership Foundation for Higher Education.

Plinske, K., Packard, W. J. (2010). Trustees' perceptions of the desired qualifications for the next generation of community college presidents. *Community College Review*, 37, 291–312. https/doi.org/10.1177/0091552109356980.

Reille, A. & Kezar, A. (2010, July). Balancing the pros and cons of community college "Grow-your-own" leadership programs. *Community College Review*, 38(1), 59–81.

Rios, J. A., Ling, G., Pugh, R., Becker, D, & Bacall, A. (2020). Identifying critical 21st century skills for workplace success: A content analysis of job advertisements. *Educational Researcher*, 49(2), 80–89.

Romano, R. M., Townsend, B., & Mamiseishvili, K. (2009). Leaders in the making: Profile and perceptions of students in community college doctoral programs. *Community College Journal of Research and Practice*, 33(3), 309–320.

Roueche, J. (1989). *Shared vision: Transformational leadership in American community colleges.* American Association of Community Colleges Press.

Schmitz, G. R. (2008). Leadership preparation and career pathways of community college presidents. [Dissertation]. Iowa State University.

Smerek, R. (2010). Sensemaking and sensegiving: An exploratory study of the simultaneous "being and learning" of new college and university presidents. Journal of Leadership & Organizational Studies, 18(1), 80–94.

Stauffer, D. C., & Maxwell, D. L. (2020). Transforming servant leadership, organizational culture, change, sustainability, and courageous leadership. *Journal of Leadership, Accountability, and Ethics*, 17(1), 105–116.

Steffens, N. K., Haslam, S. A., Reicher, S. D., Platow, M. J., Fransen, K., Yang, J., Ryan, M. K., Jetten, J., Peters, K., & Boen, F. (2014). Leadership as social identity management: Introducing the identity leadership inventory (ILI) to assess and validate a four-dimensional model. *Leadership Quarterly*, 25(5), 1001–1024. doi:10.1016/j.leaqua.2014.05.002.

Stripling, J. (2017). The profession. Characteristics of college presidents. Chronicle of Higher Education. August 18, 2017. (pp. 24-28).

Sullivan, L. G. (2001). Four generations of community college leadership. *Community College Journal of Research and Practice*, 25(4), 559–571. doi:10.1080/106689201316880759.

Sutin, S. E., Derrico, D., Raby, R. L, & Valeau, E. J. (2011). Increasing effectiveness of the community college financial model: A global perspective for the global economy. Palgrave.

Tack, M. W. (1991). Future leaders in higher education. *National Forum*, 71(1), 1–5.

Tarker, D. (2019). Transformational leadership and the proliferation of community college leadership frameworks: A systematic review of the literature. *Community College Journal of Research and Practice*. 43(10–11), 672–689. doi:10.1080/10668926.2019.1600610.

Townsend, B. K., & Bassoppo-Moyo, S. B. (1997). The effective community college academic administrator: Necessary competencies and attitudes. *Community College Review*, 25(2), 41–56. doi:10.1177/009155219702500204.

Vaughan, G. B. (1989). Black community college presidents. *Community College Review*, 17(3), 18–27. doi:10.1177/009155218901700303.

Vaughn, G. & Wiseman, I. (1998). *The community college presidency at the millennium*. The Community college Press.

Vickers, K. J. (2007). An assessment of leadership development programs for employees in Iowa community colleges. [Unpublished Doctoral Dissertation]. Iowa State University.

Vineyard, E. E. (1993a). The administrator's role in staff management. In *Managing Community Colleges: A Handbook for Effective Practice*. Edited by M. Cohen & F. Brawer, (pp. 363–381). Jossey-Bass.

Vineyard, E. E. (1993b). *The pragmatic presidency: Effective leadership in the Two-Year college*. Anker Publishing.

Wallin, D. L. (2002). Professional development for presidents: A study of community and technical college presidents in three states. *Community College Review*, 30(2), 27–41.

Weltsch, M. D. (2009). A study of community college presidential qualifications and career paths. [Unpublished Doctoral Dissertation]. Kansas State University.

Wiseman, I. M. & Vaughn, G. B. (1998). The community college presidency at the millennium. American Association of Community Colleges.

Wiseman, I. M. & Vaughn, G. B. (2002). The community college presidency, 2001. (Report No. AACC-RB-02-1; AACC Ser-3). American Association of Community Colleges.

Wiseman, I. M., & Vaughan, G. B. (2007). The community college presidency: 2006. http://www.aacc.nche.edu/Publications/Briefs/Documents/09142007presidentbrief.pdf.

Chapter Sixteen

# Keeping the Job and Performing with Distinction

In part, the literature talks about the presidency as a position of transition (Sanaghan et al., 2008; Vaughan, 2000) and strategic career decisions (Jones & Johnson, 2013). Throughout this book, the focus has been on the presidency and pathways to achieve it. However, it is essential to learn how to keep the job to prepare for the next position.

This chapter defines strategies, ideas, and thoughtfulness on keeping the job and how to perform with distinction. It is a void in the literature and may be attributable to a belief that one should instinctively know how to keep the job. It is unlikely such a conclusion is true. Too often CEOs ego and pride stand in the way of even asking the right questions about performance and vitality. Whatever the circumstances, given the amount of movement, retirements, and firings in the ranks of CEOs in todays environment, it seems timely to approach the topic on some limited basis as a step in the process of ascending to the presidency. In the end, it is what will make future leaders the most viable and may even be used to help explain their legacy.

## RULES OF KEEPING THE PRESIDENCY

I propose that specific rules will help presidents keep their position. These rules begin with using critical introspection to understanding one's philosophy, especially as it relates to expectations of self and what public image is shared to build a profile of what you want others to know about you. Shakespeare, in "Hamlet," sums it up when Polonius says, "This above all: To thine own self be true" (Shakespeare, Hamlet Act 1, Scene 3). Another rule is transparency. It is essential always to apply critical introspection to identify those who trust you to lead them and provide them with transparency so that everyone knows what to expect. A third rule in keeping the job is to learn and understand why as a leader some like you and others do not. The balance of the positive and the critical is essential because so many presidents fear losing their jobs based on what they perceive as people not liking them nor their work. The final rule to sustaining the presidency relates to the strength and courage to lose oneself while serving in the role. In this context, it is critical to focus on the importance of showing your true self to all who come before you. Thus, it is wise to have a personality assessment done on yourself to know your predispositions for conflict, work style, stress level, anxiety level, and prediction on how you might respond to the overall challenges you will undoubtedly experience throughout your tenure as president.

The Buttimer recipients and the Sitting Presidents confirm that the president is always at risk of feared things. One president shared that my personal view is "never be afraid of the job or of losing it." Another president advised to be self-assured, and feel confident that the board will claim the job back at any time, but be able to say, "Thank you for the opportunity; it is yours." While this advice sounds like a good strategy, in reality, I have rarely heard of or talked with successful presidents who publicly confess to having the attitude that if the board or the powers to be wanted their job at any time, they could have it. As a search consultant, I always asked those I was interviewing were they concerned about losing their jobs. One seasoned president shared that while they were confident and competent enough, they needed to be concerned since finding another job was not easy. Another president I was consulting, who had only been on the job for a few years, shared that they did not like being threatened with losing the job. Finally, another president that I was consulting with and looking for a new position shared that they fully understood their job, and it was not necessary or essential for them to spend the rest of their time defending who they were or what they could do. As such, in my conversations as a consultant, most seeking a new presidency position indicated that it was not worth it to work for anyone who could not see their value and appreciate its impact on successfully fulfilling the job mandate. Based on my experiences, I offer five specific strategies that will help one keep their job.

## Learn Politics

The business of the presidency is often referred to as a contact sport. It is because there are many players in the game of educational administration. Within the system, all compete for power and control to satisfy their or their constituency needs. Being able to balance these competing forces is an art form to be mastered for longevity. Cultivate friends through honesty and integrity. Show empathy and a desire to make a difference. In negotiations, strive for a win-win while accepting the fact that it is not always possible. While all politics is local, it is influenced by changing national and international winds that shape policy, mandates, and expectations frequently beyond one's control level. Learning the politics of one's environment contributes immensely to governing effectively and persuasively while building confidence in one's ability to lead, which has its reward – longevity.

## Be Competent

If one is to sustain the presidency, there is no substitute for being competent. One must know their business and what it entails (people, budget, finance, contract negotiations, fundraising, staffing, curriculum, student services, diversity, planning, bonds, and technology). These speak to the increasing number of daily expectations placed on the president. Equally important is for others as well to know that one has these competencies. In this world of challenging and changing opportunities, boards, faculty, students, and the community want and expect leaders to be influential and able to lead. Competency thus entails being omnipresent, knowing the day's issues, researching new directions for the future, and allowing oneself and others the freedom to take planned risks. The community wants to feel comfortable and assured that the person they entrusted to lead knows where they are, where they are going, and has the leadership capacity to engage them and others in understanding why and how they can achieve that next step together.

## Find Your Voice

In the *Lion King*, Simba's character perfected finding his voice, even though he was heir apparent. Having the title of the president does not make a person one. Instead, it is people's earned trust and respect that legitimates one's leadership role and style. Respect is built on being an open and honest communicator with a visible intent on listening and readiness to implement decisions. In this crucible, you can and will find your voice and have it supported. Here, you will know how to act and behave; it is here you will come to know and recognize formal and informal leaders across the organization. You will learn how to be malleable and know that many voices are just as important as one in the decision-making process, and people everywhere want in on the process both formally and informally. Ultimately though, you are the leader, and you must have confidence in leading.

### Manage Your Stress

Being able to manage stress associated with frequent criticisms is a prominent marker of resilience, courage, purpose, focus, and commitment. It assesses the patience to engage in trial and error and to be open to deep self-reflection. In this situation, one learns how to examine one's values, question one's assumptions, and meaningfully, one's judgment. In the end, it is likely you will emerge more self-assured and clearer of purpose, and as such, will be ready for the sometimes rewarding, tired, and weary journey each day in the role of the president.

### Communicate Effectively

Be consistent in professional and personal communication, and always avoid the trap of trying to be all things to all people. Understand that circumstances will govern public-private spheres. In this context, you might communicate one way to some people and another way to others, depending on the context. That said, encouraging gossip or participating in it is a misstep and is to be avoided. It is equally important never to take seriously a person who says confidently that "this is just between you and me." Such a thing does not exist, especially in our world of intensified social media. Regarding decision-making style, communicate clearly and concisely to assure a prominent competency level and a high degree of confidence in your voice. It will likely be needed to instill and motivate others' drive and energy to achieve focus, consensus, purpose, and a sense of direction.

### Continue to Learn

The world is ever-changing, and with it, knowledge. Self-development is important to sustaining the job. Start with a competent, up-to-date team that you are willing to invest in. Those who give you counsel define your ability to lead. Embrace serving others. One is fortunate to be trusted as a leader and accepted as the president of the college. Advisedly, those seeking the presidency should have a focus on diversity and an interest in knowing and learning about others. Knowing others gives you a sense of philosophy, a history of humanity, and makes you a better person. Such richness of other cultures also leads to an opportunity for others within the organization, which can only improve the institution and the students being served.

## REFERENCES

Jones, S. J., & Johnson, B. (2013). Are community college presidencies wise career moves? *Community College Journal of Research and Practice*, 38(4), 300–309.

Sanaghan, P. H., Goldstein, L., & Gaval, K. D. (2008). *Presidential transitions: It is not just the position; it is the transition*. Praeger.

Vaughan, G. B. (2000). *Balancing the presidential seesaw: Case studies in community college leadership*. AACC.

Part V

# New Directions

Chapter Seventeen

# Changing Practices and Moving the Field Forward

Community colleges have traditionally served as beacons and bridges for citizens in need of a second chance, as an alternative to the university, and as a place to gain directed skills. Universally, the community college is one of the most significant institutions globally because no matter where it is located, the community college promotes and supports the massification of higher education. In the United States, the community college is governed by multiple missions, including providing students with opportunities for continuing education, workforce training and retraining, transfer education, and lifelong learning.

On every level, the community college has and continues to face challenges from external forces that limit funding and positions it as a lesser-than institution. It faces challenges from forces inside that support a status quo and, in so doing, work to thwart efforts at real change and directly or indirectly then reinforce institutional sexism, racism, and prejudices. The conflicting nature of the community college extends to whom the community college serves. By all standards, the community college movement grew out of two competing ideologies. One purpose was not of noble thought but out of a cynical scheme to control access with the intent to keep some people out. The other purpose embraces the idea of higher education serving the public good by supporting the philosophy of open access in which the community college serves millions of students from every social class irrespective of academic preparedness, economic status, race, ethnic identity, or gender. Community college leadership, especially at the presidential level, reflects the dualities of external and internal pressures and the dualities of higher education's intent in meeting the public good and the private good.

## THE PRESIDENCY

A community college's leadership is entrusted to a President, a Chancellor, or a Superintendent/President who is held responsible for exercising leadership and authority for guiding a college or a district. Initially, community college leadership adopted university presidential leadership styles by focusing on defining responsibility and authority for accomplishing prescribed assigned duties by a governing body. Simultaneously, the early presidents were creating new constructs of leadership and pioneering new styles of leading community colleges. They became leaders of "The Little Engine That Could." Consistent development of the role has been influenced by needs and circumstances dictated by national, state, and accreditation policies, by the sociocultural and economic context of the time, and by forces within higher education that continually stress student success.

The community college serves the student. Although generally underfunded, it is tasked with the education and training of populations that have been traditionally disenfranchised and who have been denied access to the same opportunities given to students who attend universities. Under the presidents' leadership, unique curricula are added to the college offerings to better prepare students for transfer to a university, train for job opportunities, acquire lifelong learning, and build global citizenship through engagement in international education. Presidents also have a responsibility for modeling and supporting transparency and accountability in an environment where many players demand various things from more programming, better facilities, higher institutional rankings on the state, local, and national levels to infrastructure and personnel salaries. For these leaders, there are no layers of buffering.

The community college is in the community. The institution's weight is on the president's shoulder, who struggles to handle challenges related to boards of trustees, policy formation, accreditation issues, local, federal, and state mandates, policy formation, accreditation, financial stability, unionism, and community expectations. The job is complicated and overwhelming for some at times. Nevertheless, as leaders take on these roles and determine if they are the best fit, they should know that the institution demands accountability and excellence on an ongoing basis. Presidents would do well to remember that institutions do not grow old, but as people, they do. They can reinvent themselves, but their time as a leader is finite resulting in retirement brought about by aging. Occupancy of the position is a moment in time in the life of Colleges. It remains constant that presidents come and go!

## SKILL SETS

Community college leaders need to acquire specific skills and transform those skills to meet the needs of the future. The myriad of skills needed to be a president today are well documented and extends into leadership for all college areas. It requires knowledge and expert use of analytics, reporting, and decision-making far beyond the cursory level. It is critical to point out that the skill sets needed today are in themselves, limiting, as they will not meet the needs of tomorrow. For example, the AACC noted the importance of having technical skills, which focused on computer and social media literacy. These, as stand-alone skills, are essential and are fundamental in daily life. As such, the meaning of the skill is then not just with the possession of the skills. Preferably in a forward-looking construct, the future leader needs to be able to use technology and computer literacy to conduct reliable future research, extract data based on "truth," and assess trust of the data received. In this context, the leader uses technology to create meaning for institutional awareness and effective decision-making.

Another example is that AACC competencies and the literature that support the need to develop skill sets also allow future leaders to know and understand the dimensions of their organization. At a minimum, this means knowing about legal aspects of general administration, governing boards, planning, public relations, human relations, business and finance, academic and student affairs, admissions, learning resources, athletics, fundraising, and campus safety. However, in a future-looking construct, it is not enough for tomorrow's presidents to just acquire these broad skills and competencies. It will be increasingly important for future presidents to use these skills holistically to ground their vision and substantiate changes throughout the institution.

## PERSONAL FOCUS

Future leaders should quickly grasp the complexity of the president's role and the imperative of developing good coping skills. Some lessons of importance include a consistent focus on professional values versus behavior designed to sell oneself, maintenance of self-confidence, finding those even if they are smarter than you, to work with, and engage in strategic planning. More so than ever, creating a culture of trust, accountability, and transparency will promote equity and excellence for all equally. Ultimately, one of the most potent coping mechanisms is not to become a slave to the job. In challenging situations involving personal standards and values, it enables one to walk away without impunity.

### Building the Pipeline

To accelerate the needed change, presidents and their boards must become more assertive and risk-averse when recruiting candidates. They can start by making sure their recruiters are diverse and that the college requires viable and measurable cultural competency training for members of the hiring committees, including community and board members and students. Another strategy is to invest more funding to help colleges be more proactive by identifying, supporting, and sustaining diverse lower and middle managers in the pipeline. In this way, current presidents can do more to acknowledge future leadership diversity and delineate what the community can offer to candidates. Finally, boards need to focus intently on success models experienced by other community colleges to recruit racial and ethnic groups. Short of these actions, the field will continue to do the same old things and get the same results, which is unacceptable and intolerable, moving into the third decade of 2000.

## PROMOTING DIVERSITY AND EQUITY

Among all the many challenges facing community college leaders today and into the future, none is more significant than the need to accelerate its leaders' ethnic and racial makeup. In part, as the student population changes, they deserve more representative leaders. It is also precisely the diversity of leadership that brings forth new ideas and new contexts, which have long been needed to respond to the country's changing sociocultural and economic needs. More alarming is that the community college president's demographics have not changed significantly in over 20 years, and more needs to be done to improve the numbers (McFarlin et al., 1999; Stripling, 2017). Even in the 2010s, African-American, Asian and Pacific Islanders, and Latinx community, college presidents continue to be underrepresented, and in some of the most recent surveys are even showing some decline in their numbers. Despite years of talk about increasing diversity, chatter about interest in hiring from outside academe and buzz about a coming wave of retirements, college and university presidents in 2016 looked much like they did five years before (Seltzer, 2017). The percentage of minority presidents in these surveys saw only a 4% increase during the same time period when grouped together. Issues of diversity, equity, and inclusion also affect the colleges as they conduct their business and interact with stakeholders and the local community. Hoping that current research will help chart a course for the future of higher education leadership, the American Council on Education (ACE) President Molly Corbett Broad (2017) reminds those in the field that diversifying the college presidency will only continue to grow in importance. She emphasizes it is especially significant as the nation's student body grows ever more diverse.

## #BACKLIVESMATTER AND THE PRESIDENCY

John Floyds' death is a tragedy and has sparked, for now, a renewed and intensified interest in reform couched in the Black Lives Matter movement of 2020. Equally significant is the storming of the Nation' Capitol in 2021 by White Nationalist and the threat they pose to the country's democracy. What community college leaders do with these inflections is of crucial importance. Systemic racism extends into the community college's hollow halls, from curriculum to faculty and management hiring practices to upward mobility opportunities, research grants, and publishing books and articles. Eventually, it extends to student access and success. The gatekeepers at the community college are not unlike what is on the streets. It is merely a different form of policing. Nevertheless, within the system, the impact is the same for people of color.

Today, talk of reform abounds in nearly every sector of our society. While community colleges in the last few years have focused on diversity, equity, and inclusion, the notions of fairness and justice have mostly been ignored. If those in higher education choose to honor these historical inflections, I submit to community college leaders, Governing Boards, Associations, Scholars, sitting and future presidents, trustees, and doctoral students in higher education a few suggestions for focused change:

1. Establish measurable and sustainable actions to ensure that students are taught by a racially and ethnically balanced faculty representing who they are. Mandate that courses maintain an internationalized curriculum that allows students to know and appreciate the worlds' multicultural and multiethnic populations, particularly Black, Brown, and Asian contributions in this country. This act alone can improve our citizenship, empathy, and value for humanity.
2. Leaders should establish and promote a measurable institutional culture of learning and growing in a culturally, pluralistic, diverse, and dynamic internationalized environment that stresses excellence, respect, cooperation, and fairness.

3. Board of Trustees should exercise enlightened leadership and veer away from being overly concerned about their next election and fear of union backlash, and hold themselves and their campus accountable for measurable change on the focus of eliminating institutional racism. Bold leadership is the clarion call and will test their resolve to create measurable and sustainable equity policies backed by consequences.
4. Associations need to introduce new and bold, measurable, sustainable, and visionary programs that address institutional racism just as they work to address institutional budgetary needs and concerns. They should go beyond babble talk, safe, politically correct language found in their echo chambers designed to give the appearance of change while holding tight the reins on the status quo and thus their comfort zones.
5. People of Color in organizational silos, fighting for "their piece," need to abandon their suspicions of each other. They need to realize there is strength in dismantling inconvenient barriers and organizing the "one road with one belt" image to achieve equity. It can result in far more power than silo behavior and ethnic and racial politics organized to outdo one another.
6. Students need to understand the full range of power inherent in their voices. It allows them to shape and significantly influence the present and the future. Also, they need to be supported in their advocacy for change. Finally, they need to realize that being a change agent is not an easy task.

## REFERENCES

Broad, M. (2017). A joyful series of breakthroughs: An interview with Molly Broad. *Educase*, October 23. https://er.educause.edu/articles/2017/10/a-joyful-series-of-breakthroughs-an- interview-with-molly-broad.

McFarlin, C. H., Crittenden, B. J., & Ebbers, L. H. (1999). Background factors common among outstanding community college presidents. *Community College Review*, 27(3), 19–31.

Seltzer, R. (2017). College presidents diversifying slowly and growing older. *Inside Higher Education*. https://www.insidehighered.com/news/2017/06/20/college-presidents-diversifying-slowly-and-growing-older-study-finds.

Stripling, J. (2017). The profession. Characteristics of college presidents. *Chronicle of Higher Education*, August 18, 24–28.

Chapter Eighteen

# Lessons and Concluding Remarks

Aspiring leaders would do well to understand that pursuing the presidency is an arduous and sometimes lonely journey, irrespective of who you are. In the COVID-19 world, new changes made to the institution and higher education, in general, will have long-term effects. The post-COVID world will likewise have new needs for inspired leadership. As gleaned from retired and practicing leaders, there is more to the position than persistence, focus, patience, creativity, dedication, stamina, right thinking, and motivation. Instead, it is a new reenvisioning of these competencies that will move leadership into the future. The right motivation includes passion and commitment to serving students and the community, not building power and status. The exemplary dedication to being a responsible leader is to have a desire to make a difference in others' lives and have the strength to do the right thing, even when it is not popular or can get you fired. Current and future presidents need to have a strong moral compass, a code of ethical behavior in and out of the office that utilizes vision to better themselves, the college, and the community. Thus, it is imperative to answer the question: Why do I want to be a community college president? As one Sitting President concluded, if your answer to the question centers around money, prestige, and power, then it is likely that you are not a good fit for the mission and vision of community colleges of the future.

The rules that I set forth are based on my own lived experience as a CEO and a Cofounder of a national search consultant firm that helped for over two decades community colleges and districts place presidents and chancellors in their role. It also comports with participants who took part in providing information and gems of wisdom for this book.

The rules below were gained from mentoring. They were given to me by gurus in the field and at every level of college administration. Through this book, I now share them with aspiring presidents and sitting presidents to know, understand, and value their motivations for wanting to be a president, understanding the challenges of the role, and building the fortitude to make a difference.

1. You do not own the presidency. It owns you on behalf of the people who entrusted it to you until the end of your tenure, which today amounts to only a few years.
2. Appreciate every day in the office and offer thanks that you are on point to assist others in achieving success.
3. Never covet the job to the extent that you are afraid to lose it. The presidency is temporary, and as such, having an exit plan is a wise strategy.
4. Celebrate and internalize the community college's mission, vision, and values, and acknowledge its significance in making a difference in citizenry's lives.
5. Commit to continuous learning beyond your job's every day responsibilities to focus on being a world citizen.
6. Create a climate of innovation that encourages everyone in the college to honor experimentation and institutionalize trial and error goals that allow everyone to fail and succeed together.
7. Be aware of your presence. First appearances count. Many will be meeting you for the first time, and they have come to see and judge for themselves the leader.
8. Communicate openly and often, be committed to listening and above all be approachable. Know that your words carry weight.
9. Distinguish the need to avoid indecisiveness as it is the first step to destruction, but realize that waiting has tremendous value.
10. The job requires mental and physical stamina. Take care of your health as you are no use to anyone when you are ill, hobbled, or near death.
11. Being a community college president is a contact sport that requires fortitude and the courage of your convictions as a living testimony to who you are and believe yourself to be.
12. Maintain high ethical and moral standards, as this will truly define who you are long after you leave the role.
13. Be assured that the scrutiny is above the chart for presidents of color, women, and the LGBTQI+ community. Nevertheless, at the same time, understand that institutional and systemic racism comes with the territory. Avoid falling into the trap of thinking or being made to feel that you have to be better than anyone else. What you must be is competent,

comfortable in your own skin, and in what you know and are willing to learn and do.

14. Know and appreciate that you will face success, crisis, and failure every day in the presidency. Do not let that deter you from your vision to assist others in achieving success. What is most important is not what happened, but your demeanor in handling the situation. That is what you and others will most remember.
15. Avoid analysis paralysis as it will assuredly stifle creativity but always seize the advantage of the moment.
16. Accept your flaws but constantly work to change them while remembering to appreciate that you are human.

Preparation for tomorrow's presidency is significantly different from yesteryears, but still rests on proven and sound foundations. The literature, coupled with current and previous occupants' wisdom, reveals that continuous focused learning through the occupation of various roles in the organization is fertile ground for what a president will encounter. If aspirants are observant, mindful, intentional, and patient, they can learn a great deal and respect doing their job. All of the competencies mentioned in this book are important. Below are nuggets that have served me the best in ascending to the Superintendent/President's role and contributed to my competencies and fit to serve.

1. Have the desire and acquire an internalized understanding of the role.
2. Obtain the critical and relevant experiences needed to do the job, including a doctorate degree.
3. Master knowledge about all the skills for the position and embrace lifelong learning.
4. Know how to use data critically, but also be open to what that data might reveal unexpectedly to enhance your knowledge about educational trends.
5. Secure a mentor(s).
6. Cultivate a strong network.
7. Put students first.
8. Cultivate relationships across sectors to support the institution by being the community college spokesperson who supports the community agenda.
9. Perform with distinction and with ethical behavior as part of the rules of the road.
10. Promote diversity as a way to meet a founding principle of the community college mission – that of access, success equity, and justice.

## CONCLUDING REMARKS

The road to the presidency has long been shrouded in mystery, particularly for those new to the position's internal workings. There are many ways to get to the presidency, albeit traditionally it has gone through the academic pipeline and more recently through student services. As new talent emerges from different sectors of the work world, and more racial and ethnic groups are recruited and employed, there is a small but shifting trend to where presidents come from nontraditional pathways. They include law, business, manufacturing, medicine, and the clergy, to name a few. The words of advice given to me and shared in this book are not intended to fit all. However, I am convinced they do give aspirants a deeper understanding of some proven footsteps to the presidency.

I hope that after reading this book, aspiring leaders will have discovered or have affirmed that there is no mystery to becoming a community college president. While it is undoubtedly influenced by time, space, and human behavior, and some luck, it is attainable by those who desire and commit to pursue the journey and acquire the needed preparation to sit in the role. It is also ground in understanding and accepting the importance of championing community college ideals, a critical insight into understanding how to mobilize stakeholders to act on behalf of the college, and understanding how to use all the communications resources available to connect with the college community.

The community college presidency is a noble profession and is quite rewarding for those who choose to serve. Expectedly, the challenges are many, especially as the sociocultural, political, and economic climates become more intense and tumultuous. The post-COVID world has surfaced new changes that all aspiring leaders will need to acknowledge. There are no shortcuts for reaching the top. The road at times is long and the seat lonely at times. Nevertheless, leaders who are fortunate to reach the top will find the job to be an enriching, satisfying career full of possibilities and rewards that exceeds financial gains, power, and prestige. They will discover the power of the presidency in influencing and shaping people's lives, thus making an informed citizenry prepared to take on the societal challenges of the 21st century and beyond.

Finally, I want to end with a Chinese parable to demonstrate the importance of teamwork and leadership in helping people see themselves as part of a broader community for everyone's success. It particularly relates to students, institutional and Community success, and the president's role as head of the college.

There was a man whom one night had dreams in which he first visited hell and then heaven. He found himself in a vast banquet hall in the first dream where many people gathered around great tables laden with food. Their problem was that the chopsticks they had been given to use were so long that it was impossible to use them to lift the food to their mouths. The people were becoming increasingly angry and frustrated in their efforts to reach the food. In the second dream, he found himself in a hall the same as in the first dream with steaming hot food tables. However, in this dream, each person chopsticks were used to lift the food to the person's mouth, sitting across the table. In this way, all enjoyed the banquet.

# Epilogue

"Leaders become leaders by being leaders." program guide, Community College Leadership Program, the University of Texas at Austin.

Over the last six decades, the role of the community college CEO has undergone transformational change. That change reflects transformation within the institutions themselves as they sought to respond to societal, economic, cultural, and demographic factors. From the explosive growth of the 1960s to meet the high demand for postsecondary access, the colleges have continued to reinvent themselves to meet the needs of the communities they serve and an increasingly expanding and diverse student body.

The question of what these transformations portend for community college leaders going forward is at the heart of Dr. Edward Valeau's current work. In his painstakingly researched Guide, Dr. Valeau mines an impressive body of scholarship focused on two-year colleges and their leaders. He chronicles not only the generational evolution of the community college CEO but also the historical context that fostered such continuous change. It is an ambitious undertaking and provides an important new resource for aspiring college leaders and a refresher course for sitting presidents and others who are dedicated to the two-year college mission. Of particular note is his original survey and analysis of Buttimer Award recipients, CEOs recognized for excellence within the California Community College System, the nation's largest.

Since an epilogue is, by definition, a look forward that amplifies the central topic, my comments offer a projection of the community college CEO's role in the 21st century. They are based on my personal and professional journey: more than four decades in community college administration – as a first-time college president, a state system leader, a university administrator, and the CEO of a national educational association.

What do we see on the horizon for community college presidents? First, it is not a job for the faint of heart! Today's president must know more, do more, and constantly anticipate. He or she can expect to spend much more time outside the campus setting – fundraising, friend-raising, and advocating. As traditional funding sources dwindle, there is a constant need to tap into added resources, innovate, and create new partnerships that leverage existing capacity. Technology is pervasive, and the CEO must know how, when, and where to invest. Further, today's and tomorrow's leader must understand the power of ever-changing technological advances and deploy that power to maintain a competitive edge and demonstrable outcomes. These skill sets may not be routinely part of many leadership programs and academic and professional development options.

Dr. Valeau's Guide cites numerous sources that seek to define the professional and personality traits of the successful CEO. Included is the American Association of Community Colleges' AACC Competencies for Community College Leaders, which has been exceptionally well received by colleges, professional development programs, and governing boards. The document has recently been revised to consider the student success agenda and more nuanced operational environments. The publication is structured to provide an objective guide, not only for CEOs but also for aspiring leaders at all levels.

Although there are some commonalities, the varied lists of desired presidential characteristics and skillsets detailed in the Guide show just how difficult it is to define, much less prepare, the "perfect" community college president. Little wonder that boards and search committees increasingly must choose from a narrowing field of CEO candidates.

At this writing, we cannot say with certainty if or when the virtual tsunami of community college CEO retirements that have substantially increased demand for new leaders will recede. An unfortunate by-product of higher demand can sometimes translate into candidates who find themselves rushed too soon into leadership roles for which they are ill-prepared. Such a situation shortchanges both the individual and the institution and can result in considerable financial and reputational cost to the hiring institution and concomitant damage to the presidential candidate's career.

However, I choose to see the challenge of building a robust leadership pipeline as a glass half full, not half empty. As Dr. Valeau notes in his book, increased presidential turnover suggests "an unprecedented opportunity to reconsider community college leadership through fresh lenses." Suppose we are to "reimagine the community college of the future," as AACC's 2012 report from the 21st Century Commission on the Future of Community Colleges recommends. In that case, we must also aspire to identify – and prepare – leaders who come to the role with both traditional and expanded competencies. It is critically important that they also better reflect the diversity of our students, our colleges, and our nation.

AACC and others such as the American Council on Education, the Aspen Institute, and the League for Innovation in the Community College continue to sponsor a range of quality leadership development opportunities. AACC's Future Leaders Institute and Future Presidents Institute have "graduated" well over 1,200 candidates since their inception. The Association's annual convention has grown as a fertile leadership "classroom" with the addition of a New CEO Academy and a mentoring component that pairs new CEOs with seasoned CEOs for the event. I find it personally rewarding to host a convention discussion that allows me to "take a pulse" by directly engaging with new CEOs about pressing issues. In addition, the annual Presidents Academy Summer Institute continues to thrive as a forum that welcomes CEOs at all levels of experience.

No forecast of leadership challenges ahead would be complete without an examination of an issue AACC considers a moral imperative: student equity. For too many community college students, achievement gaps persist, and students do not attain the education and skills needed to enter the workforce and earn family-sustaining wages. What AACC is terming Unfinished Business is now a major focus for the Association and will require the active engagement of community colleges for the near future. Those who lead our colleges must ask themselves if only certain types of students succeed, can we truly be the accessible, inclusive institutions our mission demands and our students deserve.

*Dr. Walter G. Bumphus*
*President and CEO, American Association of Community Colleges*

# Index

Note: **Bold** page numbers refer to tables and *italic* page numbers refer to figures

Printed in the United States
by Baker & Taylor Publisher Services